AS Film Studies
UNIT 3

WJEC

Unit FS3: Messages and Values

Tanya Jones

AYLESBURY COLLEGE
LEARNING CENTRE

Philip Allan Updates
Market Place
Deddington
Oxfordshire
OX15 0SE

Tel: 01869 338652
Fax: 01869 337590
e-mail: sales@philipallan.co.uk
www.philipallan.co.uk

© Philip Allan Updates 2004

ISBN-13: 978-0-86003-927-3
ISBN-10: 0-86003-927-7

This Guide has been written specifically to support students preparing for the WJEC Film Studies Unit 3 examination. The content has been neither approved nor endorsed by WJEC and remains the sole responsibility of the authors.

Printed by MPG Books, Bodmin

Environmental information
The paper on which this title is printed is sourced from managed, sustainable forests.

P00679

AS Film Studies

Contents

Introduction

■ ■ ■

Content Guidance

■ ■ ■

Questions and Answers

Introduction

About this guide

This unit guide is for students following the WJEC AS Film Studies course. It deals with **Unit FS3: Messages and Values**, which is designed to test your ability to discuss messages and values within film examples from British and Irish cinema. There are three sections to this guide.

- **Introduction** — this provides advice on how to use the guide, an explanation of the skills required for the exam, an outline of the exam structure, guidance on writing exam essays and suggestions on how to revise effectively.
- **Content Guidance** — this explains the skills and outlines the content you will need to cover in the exam. It uses examples from both the comparative study (section A) and the single film close study (section B) components of the unit to illustrate how these skills can be applied.
- **Questions and Answers** — this provides exam-style questions and answers for both section A and section B. The answers are at grade-A and grade-C level. They are accompanied by examiner's comments, which explain how the marks are awarded. A selection of essay titles for revision and practice is included too.

How to use the guide

To get the maximum possible benefit from this guide, use it systematically. Make sure you read through the whole of the Introduction carefully, taking full note of the exam skills, exam structure and revision tips offered. When you have a thorough overview of the skills needed and the format of the exam, you should move on to the Content Guidance section.

This section covers the skills and content areas for Unit 3. It explains the skills fully and uses examples from both the comparative study and the single film close study elements of the exam to illustrate how these can be applied. It would be extremely useful for you to make notes on your chosen texts, using your experience as a consumer of those texts, as you read through this section.

When you have completed your study of the essential skills and content, you should then move on to look at the Question and Answer section. Here you will find examples of types of exam question. Each question is followed by two answers, one of which is grade-A standard and one of which is grade-C standard. Take note of the structure of the best answers, as well as the information they contain. Make sure that you read the examiner's comments on each answer too, noting the features of the answers that are praised and the possible pitfalls.

The Unit 3 specification

This unit focuses on how messages and values are generated in film examples from British and Irish cinema. The micro and macro analysis skills you gained during your FS1: Film — Making Meaning 1 coursework, and the knowledge of the British film industry that you gained during your preparation for FS2: Producers and Audiences, will be useful.

Unit 3 requires you to evaluate how messages and values are generated in specific film texts and how they are received by the viewer of those texts. You will need to have a good understanding of representation in order to do well in this exam. Your ability to use close textual analysis when discussing representation is the key to success in this exam, as is your ability to comment on how historical and social contexts inform representations.

The specification for this unit emphasises the importance of students using their own experiences to inform their comment on particular texts. You should do this in two ways. First, your experiences of your film studies course so far should be used in your analysis of both text and context. Second, your own experience as a consumer of texts can be used in discussion of the impact of messages and values on the film audience.

Examinable skills

There are four main skills you need to demonstrate in the Unit 3 exam. These are an ability to:

- identify messages and values, both explicit and implicit, in films
- critically evaluate representation within film texts
- contextualise films, both historically and socially
- reflect on your personal response to a film's messages and values

To exhibit the first of these skills in your examination answer, you need to discuss the ideas and the ideology evident within your chosen film(s). The film(s) you are studying will discuss various social or national groups through the representation of characters, settings, cinematography, *mise-en-scène* and even editing. You need to discern what kinds of comments a film offers explicitly, through dialogue, and also the implicit comments offered through representation, and micro and macro elements. You may find contradictions between what the film seems to be saying explicitly and implicitly. For example, the characters might express a certain attitude towards being a member of a particular social or national group, but the context in which they are placed and the camerawork used might indicate a contradictory stance. In this situation it is essential to identify the contradiction and then discuss why the characters' and the film's attitudes to a certain issue seem to be contradictory.

Representations

An understanding of representation is vital in identifying the messages and values contained in the films you are studying. Representation is the process by which a word, image or sound is given meaning beyond that which it initially appears to have. The word, image or sound comes to indicate an idea or a debate. The most common form of representation is that of social groups. You need to consider whether or not you think the representation of a particular group is intentional.

You should analyse both the positive and negative aspects of representation in the film(s) you are studying. Whether a particular representation is seen as positive or negative is subjective, and different members of a social group might have opposing views of what is or is not a positive or negative representation. You also need to decide whether you think a group is being represented in a stereotypical way, or whether a stereotype is being challenged.

Textual elements

Your ability to evaluate representation critically depends on your ability to analyse all of the textual factors that contribute towards the construction of representation in a text. The characters' dialogue, plus their narrative positioning, as well as the *mise-en-scène*, cinematography, sound and editing associated with these characters, will help you decide what is being said about a particular social group.

Contextual elements

Analysis of the social and historical contexts of a film is important in discussing representation fully. There might have been particular events that occurred, or social attitudes that were dominant, in the years surrounding a film's release, and these could have had a significant impact on the representational aspects of that film. *Local Hero* (Forsyth, 1983), for example, is set in the 1980s, when individualism and conspicuous consumption were seen as synonymous with young, upwardly mobile, professionals. The film explores this lifestyle through its main character, a Porsche-driving, affluent, young American man, who visits a rural Scottish community and then rejects his previous value system in favour of the community spirit the Scottish village seems to offer. *Local Hero* therefore represents a lifestyle driven by consumerism as hollow, challenging the value system common to a significant number of people in the 1980s.

Ideology

Ideology is the system of ideas, values and beliefs that are held as important by an individual, group or society. The term 'ideology' describes a set of shared beliefs, which can include attitudes to class, race, sexual orientation and gender. A dominant ideology is a set of ideas held by the majority: it can affect the way an individual responds to a film or the types of story, character and image seen within a film. If the dominant ideology at a particular point in history was that women had less status than men, for example, then an ideological study of the films produced at that time would show whether these dominant social attitudes had influenced the work of film makers. Your study of ideology will form an essential part of your discussion of representation, because the way in which a group is represented will illustrate the ideology discussed in the film.

Hegemony is the process by which a dominant ideology is maintained. It is created initially by powerful institutions such as the government, the mass media, religion or the family. The ideas that come from these institutions become the most powerful, and are maintained through their inclusion in media products such as film. Audiences for these media products might challenge the ideology within them or they might accept it as true. In your film analysis, you should identify the ideologies that are evident and decide whether these represent dominant social attitudes or whether such attitudes are being challenged.

Personal responses

The final skill required by this unit is an ability to reflect on your personal response to a film's messages and values. Once you have discussed the ideology indicated by a film's representational elements, you need to discuss your own reaction to the messages and values evident. Do you consider a group's representation as challenging stereotypes or reinforcing them? Do you agree with the ideology that is apparent within your film? You should consider the similarities and differences between your own responses to a film and those of critics.

The exam

Unit 3 is worth 30% of the AS marks and 15% of the whole A-level grade. The exam lasts 90 minutes, and is split into two sections. You are required to answer one question from each section. The distribution of marks for this paper is not balanced — section A questions carry 35 marks and section B questions carry 25 marks. You should allocate your time in the exam accordingly, spending 50 minutes on section A and 40 minutes on section B.

Section A examines the comparative study, and contains two questions for each of the six topics on the specification. When you open your exam paper, you should turn straight to the topic that you have studied in your lessons and answer one of the questions. No matter how attractive another topic's questions look to you, you should never attempt to answer a question on a topic that you have not studied fully. The same applies to section B, which covers the single film close study. It includes three question options, from which you should select the one focusing on the film you have studied in class.

Writing an exam essay

There are several factors to consider when you are sitting an exam: question choice, your approach to the question, and — an element that is often forgotten under pressure — the structure and style of your writing. Make sure that you practise writing under timed conditions, to ensure that you can structure answers in a clear, comprehensive and systematic way. The areas to consider when writing both comparative study and single film close analysis essays are outlined below.

Planning

It is important to organise your essay before you commence writing. This can be done using a series of bullet points that list the areas to be covered in your essay. You should also make a brief note of any textual or contextual examples you are going to include. Reject or rephrase any point for which you cannot think of an example, and cross off each point as you write about it. Don't forget to plan for time to read through your work when you have finished writing. You can often avoid spelling and grammatical errors with a final read-through.

Introduction and conclusion

Your essay must have a clear introduction and conclusion. The introduction should address the question specifically and describe the particular approach that you are offering. The conclusion should offer a summary of your argument and should not introduce new points.

Developing your argument

Between your introduction and conclusion should be a systematic and relevant development of your ideas. Make sure that each paragraph feeds into the next — examiners do not want to read disjointed pieces of writing. Avoid repetition and make sure that whatever you write is fully substantiated by references to textual or contextual detail.

It is important that your essay is structured appropriately. In your comparative study essay you will be analysing a group of topic-related films. Your focus film will call for more comment than the others, but you should be careful to grant your comparative films enough coverage to substantiate the main ideas of your essay. In your single film close study essay you will be analysing one text closely. When answering either section A or section B questions, there are key points to remember:

- Be specific in your references and don't waffle.
- Always substantiate your points with reference to examples.
- Don't merely regurgitate received opinion. Use your own readings to challenge others.
- Make sure that your line of argument is clear to your examiner.

Paragraph structure

Remember to use paragraphs — clarity of argument is always lost when you adopt a 'stream of consciousness' style of writing. The paragraphs that make up the main body of your essay need to be structured carefully. Below is a suggested method of organising paragraphs that will help you create coherent essays:

(1) Open with a statement that identifies the point you are trying to make.

(2) Follow this with a clear textual or contextual example.

(3) Next, you should elaborate on your original statement.

(4) To close the paragraph, try to refer to the viewer or audience's response to the issue you have raised.

This method is applied to the examples that follow.

Comparative study paragraph example

(1) The film *Local Hero* offers two varying representations of life in the 1980s.

(2) Mac's life in Houston revolves around money and conspicuous consumption, whereas the villagers in Scotland seem to value community and self-reliance.

(3) This difference in value systems is what creates the tensions and developments in the film.

(4) The viewer is offered a comment on the loneliness that can be born out of a purely money-orientated mindset, as well as the community spirit that can be fostered by a group of people pursuing one goal.

Single film close study paragraph example

(1) The representation of family is a key area to consider in Mike Leigh's 1996 film, *Secrets and Lies*.

(2) The film follows Hortense's quest to find her birth mother.

(3) Families in this film challenge the stereotypical representation of the nuclear family, as they are characterised by absence and conflict.

(4) For the viewer, the representation of family offered is one that seems to mirror contemporary society more accurately than the nuclear stereotype.

Terminology

You should use specific film-related terminology where appropriate. Do not clutter your essay with too many terms, but do use them where applicable and only if you know exactly what they mean. Using terms such as narrative, genre, *mise-en-scène* and iconography will give a clear indication that you know what you are talking about.

Study skills and revision strategies

The golden rule of revision is not to leave it until just before your exam. You should begin to prepare for the exam from the outset of your AS course. If you organise your

notes from the beginning, you will not have to waste time sifting through them close to the exam date. Always keep your notes in one or more folders, with dividers indicating each topic.

Within the different sections, highlight key words or terms. Your notes should also include clear definitions of terms, such as representation and ideology, which you will need for the exam.

Content revision will take up a significant proportion of your exam preparation time. However, it is vital to practise writing under timed conditions, and to become accustomed to allocating 50 minutes for section A and 40 minutes for section B. Use the Question and Answer section to pick up tips on organising your answer, and ask your teacher for past exam papers to practise on. A list of questions you can use for practice is included at the end of the Question and Answer section (pp. 62–63).

If you begin the revision process early in your course, by rereading your notes and adding personal examples, then you will avoid having to rush at a later date. Asking questions in class and rereading your notes after lessons will ensure that information stays with you, and you will be able to approach your revision in a relaxed and confident manner.

Content
Guidance

This section begins by offering guidance on analysing representations in films, including textual, contextual and ideological aspects, to find messages and values. This is followed by details of the content required for section A, the comparative study, and then for section B, the single film close study. The notes you have made in class should be used alongside this information.

Guidance on the comparative study component is divided into the following areas:
- How to approach the comparative study
- The 1940s: the war and its aftermath
- Swinging Britain, 1963–73
- Passions and repressions
- Social and political conflict
- Scottish cinema
- Comedy

The single film close study aspect is covered as follows:
- How to approach the single film close study
- Case study 1: *Secrets and Lies*
- Case study 2: *Elizabeth*
- Case study 3: *Chicken Run*

Films that have an 18 certificate have been identified with an asterisk. The WJEC Film Studies AS specification allows the use of 18-certified films. Your teacher will advise you of their suitability for study purposes.

Section A: the comparative study

How to approach the comparative study

The comparative study element of the Unit 3 exam requires you to analyse a group of films that have been linked together under a specific topic heading. Whether this topic is comedy, Scottish cinema or any of the other options, the analytical process is the same. It involves evaluating representation within your chosen films and the textual and contextual factors that have created these representations.

You might find representations of class, gender, sexuality, religion, race, or regional or national identity in a film or you might decide that it is a social institution, such as the family, or a political institution, such as the legal system, which is being represented. In addition, your essay should comment on the social and historical contexts of a film and how they have influenced the film's representations.

There are six comparative study topic areas; your teacher will decide on the topic area you will study. For each topic area there is a designated focus film, which you must study and comment on in the exam. Your teacher will also select films in addition to the focus text, which you will use in your analysis. Your focus film will provide the foundation of your analysis of representation, but you should make sure that you refer to the other films in some detail, comparing how their representations relate to your focus film and to the wider topic area.

Key words

analysis; representation; stereotype; social context; historical context; ideology; hegemony; class; gender; sexuality; religion; race; regional identity

The 1940s: the war and its aftermath

This topic requires you to consider issues of representation in films that were made during the Second World War and films made after the war, up until the end of the 1940s. Your study of representation could consider gender, nationality, class, power, authority or community. You also need to evaluate how the messages and values that you identify within your films relate to those that were important during the period in which the films were made.

The focus films for this particular topic are *Went the Day Well?* (Calvalcanti, 1942) and *Fires Were Started* (Jennings, 1943).

Messages and values

There are various debates that you could use in your discussions of the war and its aftermath. If your films were made during the war, then they might articulate a

direct wartime experience. If your films were made after the war was over, then they will probably be concerned with reconstruction — both the economic reconstruction of the UK and the reconstruction of the individual and national psyche. You need to consider to what extent the films made during the Second World War helped to foster a sense of national solidarity or whether, in contrast, they aimed to articulate the internal conflicts within the UK at that time. The issue of class might be significant within your films and you should consider how class divisions are represented, as well as how different classes of people are seen to respond to wartime conditions.

In addition, you might be able to evaluate the impact of war and wartime restrictions on the family unit. Your films might focus on different regions of Britain and if this is the case, then a study of the different representations attached to different regions of Britain would be necessary. You might have studied films that depict both a rural and an urban context and thus you would be able to consider the different responses that the inhabitants of these areas have to the war.

Focus film: *Went the Day Well?*

Went the Day Well? is the story of the invasion of a remote village by a group of undercover German troops posing as Royal Engineers. The film plots the mounting tensions and accusations as the inhabitants become suspicious of the undercover soldiers. The film discusses the impact of suspicion and fear of being invaded within the context of a remote village, but illustrates the wider social fears of wartime Britain about the German threat. Cavalcanti presents the viewer with a traditional image of the British village, including pub, post office and church, and community-spirited villagers. What is perhaps most interesting about this film, however, is the impact of the anti-German fervour ignited by the discovery of the invading forces. The once sedate village becomes a hotbed of violent thoughts and the discovery that the village's community leader is a traitor provokes reactions from the villagers that would previously have seemed unbelievable. Scenes of a peaceful rural idyll are replaced by the end of the film with housewives killing German troops with what seems to be real enthusiasm. As a discussion of the dehumanisation of war, the film seems to suggest that dehumanisation is not only apparent within those who are trained to kill.

Comparative films

Passport to Pimlico

Passport to Pimlico (Cornelius, 1949) depicts the aftermath of the Second World War and its impact not only on the environment but also on the psyche of a community. The film was released at a time when the British public was still experiencing the hardships of rationing. The inhabitants of Pimlico believe they have found evidence that they are an independent state and should therefore not be governed by British laws. They set up a restriction-free state in which rationing does not exist. Within economically stricken Britain, this eventually proves unworkable, and the independent state is forced to resort to rationing of its own. *Passport to Pimlico* is an Ealing comedy and employs comic characterisation and comic scenarios to offer its messages. The film has serious points to make, however, concerning the true nature of independence. The 'free' state of Pimlico is initially a place of euphoria and post-war indulgence, yet by the end of the film it becomes as dominated by hierarchy and sanctions as any other country.

Further suggestions

Other films that you could include in your discussion are:

- *Next of Kin* (Dickinson, 1942)
- *The Life and Death of Colonel Blimp* (Powell, 1943)
- *A Matter of Life and Death* (Powell/Pressburger, 1946)
- *Hue and Cry* (Crichton, 1947)

Key words

gender; nationality; class; power; authority; community; wartime experience; reconstruction; individual/national psyche; national solidarity; rural context; urban context; dehumanisation

Swinging Britain, 1963–73

This topic area asks you to consider the period often referred to as the 'swinging sixties'. The 10-year span to be studied includes the first few years of the 1970s and allows you to consider films that were released during this period. The focus films for this topic are *A Hard Day's Night* (Lester, 1964) and *Darling* (Schlesinger, 1965).

Messages and values

There are various ways in which this topic can be approached. Try to begin with the term 'swinging Britain'. Was Britain 'swinging' for everybody or just for a small section of society? The notion of a 'swinging' London and its difference from the rest of the country might be a matter of debate within your films. Once you have a definition, you should use your group of films to debate whether the cultural and social revolutions said to have occurred from 1963–73 were real or merely a construction. If you consider the revolutions to be constructed, you need to identify who constructed them and why.

The 1960s are often portrayed as a time in which artistic freedom reigned and individuals left the oppression of the more conservative 1950s behind. You could analyse the cultural pursuits of individuals and the changing fashions in music, art, literature and cinema. Consider whether your films seem to chart changing patterns in taste and cultural experiences, and try to evaluate whether you consider the 10 years of the topic's title as a significant time for social and cultural development.

You might look at how the representations of youth and class are constructed in your chosen films and consider to what extent these mirrored actual, prevalent social attitudes. The representation of gender will be significant, too, particularly in a period that is often deemed to have been the time of a sexual revolution.

Whether you choose films that discuss individual freedom or the social problems of the period, or whether you focus on those films that have caused controversy, you will need to evaluate the messages and values presented in these films against what you learn about the dominant social attitudes.

Focus film: *A Hard Day's Night*

A Hard Day's Night presents a number of themes for discussion, which would have been evident in social debate at the time the film was made. Age and class are included in the representations of this film and you need to consider whether stereotypes are invoked in order to present the Beatles in a particular light to their fans. The gap between the experiences and pre-occupations of youth and age is discussed in the film through the conflict that the group has with the figures of authority around them. The representation of those characters who stand for 'age' is mixed. The character of Norm does his best to keep the group out of trouble, but ironically it is the character of John Lennon's grandfather who creates the most problematic situations. *A Hard Day's Night* seems to present youth (in the form of the Beatles) as anarchic and disrespectful of traditional social divides. The Beatles are seen in various playful scenes, in which they seem to conflict with authority. However, although they may be playful and at times irresponsible, they are not completely devoid of responsibility. Youth is not portrayed as being completely without sense and the social fear of the morality-free teenager is challenged by the antics of the group members and the older characters around them.

As a 'pop' film, *A Hard Day's Night* is in essence a promotional piece that seeks to present the group in a way that is most attractive and palatable to the group's fans. The young girls who constitute the majority of the Beatles' fanbase are presented with young men who are exuberant and anti-authoritarian. These young men, however, are not seen in contexts related to either sex or drugs and you need to consider this when you are discussing whether the representations of youth and pop musicians are accurate or sanitised.

The Beatles are presented as working-class boys made good. They do not adhere to traditional class divides, as is evident during the scene on the train where they encounter social snobbery, but they do represent a new social phenomenon: the cult of pop. *A Hard Day's Night* is as much a discussion of 'Beatlemania' and the birth of a new social 'class' (the rich, young pop musician) as it is a discussion of youth and age. The film fuses a documentary style of cinematography with scenes of choreographed madcap behaviour in order to comment on the 'Beatlemania' that was sweeping Britain at the time the film was made.

Comparative films

A Clockwork Orange*

Your study for this topic may include analysis of films that caused controversy and created debate. Stanley Kubrick's 1971 film *A Clockwork Orange** certainly fits these criteria. In 1971, the British Board of Film Classification had passed the film with an X certificate and it was being shown in the UK, but Kubrick withdrew it from circulation in 1972. This was the result of pressure from groups such as the Festival of Light, an organisation that aimed to purge Britain of what it deemed to be immoral influences, and which campaigned vigorously for the film to be banned. This pressure, together with the attacks on the film by religious groups, the *Daily Mail*'s campaign against it, and the naming of the film as a contributory factor in various crimes of the period, led to Kubrick's decision. The ban continued until Kubrick's death in 1999.

A Clockwork Orange* offers an interesting case study of the conflicting social attitudes of the time. The film follows the events in the life of Alex, who leads his 'droogs' into crimes of rape and murder before he is caught. The aversion therapy that Alex experiences after his capture was a cause of great debate in the 1960s and 1970s. The film represents this therapy as dehumanising and barbaric.

Criticism of the film revolved around the representation of authority figures, such as politicians and doctors, as being almost as violent as Alex and the 'droogs' had been. The fact that the audience is guided through the film by a voiceover from Alex led critics to be concerned that viewers were expected to empathise with him and his actions. You would need to debate whether or not you consider the representation of youth in the film (as exemplified by Alex) to be less negative than the representation of the authority figures.

Further suggestions

Other films that could contribute to a comparative study on this period are:
- *Alfie* (Gilbert, 1966)
- *Georgy Girl* (Narizzano, 1966)
- *If...* (Anderson, 1968)
- *Performance** (Cammel/Roeg, 1970)

Key words

social/cultural/sexual revolution; youth; age; class; 'pop' film; anti-authoritarianism; controversy

Passions and repressions

The focus of this topic is the representation of sexuality and desire in specific social contexts. This could mean an analysis of passions and repressions within films that centre on specific social classes, range across different social classes or focus on a

social unit, such as the family. You might consider the representation of homosexuality, for example in *My Beautiful Laundrette* (Frears, 1985), and analyse the ways in which sexuality is repressed in order to conform to social norms. The focus film for this topic is either *Brief Encounter* (Lean, 1945) or *Beautiful Thing* (MacDonald, 1996).

Messages and values

Whichever films you choose for a comparative study of passions and repressions, you should begin by deconstructing the two words in the topic title carefully. Consider what type of passion is being expressed within your film and what the cause of the repression might be. Is it desire that is being repressed, or is desire the only avenue of expression left for characters who have been repressed by their social situation and the attitudes of those around them? Remember to consider the dominant ideologies that existed at both the time your film was made and at the time it was set, and evaluate how this ideological context has informed or influenced your film.

The key areas of debate for this topic often revolve around a central dynamic. You might consider the relationship between sex and class, for example, or the relationship between sex and race. You could consider the time in which the film was made or the time it depicts, and analyse how social attitudes towards sex and class or sex and race are discussed in your films. Consider whether representation within the films you have chosen conforms to the dominant social attitudes of the time or whether the messages and values in your films are more subversive.

Focus film: *Brief Encounter*

David Lean's *Brief Encounter* deals with passions and repressions within the same social class. It tells the story of an affair between Laura and Alec. They are both upper-middle class and are supposedly happily married to other people. Neither character plans to have an affair, and both are surprised by the strength of feeling that they have for each other. The story of their encounter is told through a voice-over from Laura, and it is thus delivered to the audience by a subjective voice. The events shown in the film are Laura's version and the viewer must consider this when evaluating the reliability of the events portrayed. Laura is telling the story retrospectively and her words are therefore saturated by the feelings of love and guilt that the encounter produced.

The ideological context of the film informs its messages and values. The affair is not a sexual one — the film was made in 1945 and post-war Britain was not ready for a tale of sexual liaison. The betrayal within the film is emotional, rather than physical, and the encounter is 'brief' because both characters decide to do what they consider to be morally and socially appropriate, and return to their respective spouses. Laura cannot bring herself to leave behind her socially acceptable position of wife and mother. She is seen as having little authority in her relationship with her husband and little in relation to the other male characters she encounters in the film. Her representation does not challenge the dominant social attitude of the 1940s towards women and their place in society, and her inability to leave her socially validated life confirms her passive role.

There is a pervasive sense of guilt and shame throughout the film, even outside of what Laura says in her voice-over. The passion that the characters feel for each other is deemed unacceptable for both the characters and the narrative, and the repression of these feelings is shown to be both inevitable and socially 'right'. The characters in *Brief Encounter* at once represent English restraint and the dominant ideologies concerning the family unit.

Comparative films

The Remains of the Day

The Remains of the Day (Ivory, 1993) presents a class-related context for passions and repressions, too. The narrative focus of the film is the relationship between Stevens and Miss Kenton, who are servants in a stately home. They are from the working class and yet live their lives within an upper-class environment. The film is set in the years before the Second World War and describes a scenario in which English sensibilities and restraint have become extreme. Stevens has an unquestioning, and misjudged, respect for the opinions and values of his master. His life is wholly consumed by his role and he is unable to engage with the potential affection offered by Miss Kenton. The scene in which she finds him reading a romantic novel is a key sequence in Stevens's representation. He can neither admit to having romantic thoughts nor respond to her advances. The repression of his character is a result of his inability to break out of his rigid notion of social roles. He does not articulate his passions like the characters in *Brief Encounter*, but does conform to the same kind of social conditioning which means that Laura and Alec's relationship is short-lived.

Letter to Brezhnev

If your focus is the analysis of passions and repressions across different social classes, then Chris Bernard's 1985 film *Letter to Brezhnev* might provide a suitable contrast with a film like *Brief Encounter*. *Letter to Brezhnev* is set in Liverpool and tells the story of two working-class women who, in their desire to escape the tedium of unemployment in one case, and a chicken factory in the other, go for a night out in Liverpool and meet two Russian sailors. The character of Teresa has no illusions about the union she has with her sailor. She sleeps with him and then returns to the factory, unable to see a life outside her daily drudgery. Elaine, on the other hand, begins to see a different life for herself — maybe even in Russia.

The characters in this film do not repress their passions and indeed use them in order to escape from their dull lives. The repression of the film is economic, as the women are trapped by their lack of money and career prospects. For these two women, 1980s Britain is not a time of individual wealth and opportunity. They are diametrically opposite to the 'yuppy' culture. The Thatcher dream of independent financial gain is not possible for these women. Liverpool is presented as grim and impoverished. It can offer little more to these women than a night out with sailors.

Further suggestions

You could also consider the following films:

- *Victim* (Dearden, 1961)
- *My Beautiful Laundrette* (Frears, 1985)
- *The Magic Toyshop* (Wheatley, 1987)
- *Sammy and Rosie Get Laid* (Frears, 1987)

Key words

sexuality; desire; social context; ideological context; class; social unit; homosexuality; race; English sensibilities/restraint; social conditioning

Social and political conflict

This topic addresses issues of representation in films dealing with social and/or political conflict. Films suitable for this area might deal with situations of ideological confrontation, racial conflict or social injustice, for example. The focus films are *It Happened Here* (Bronlow/Mollo, 1966) and *Bloody Sunday* (Greengrass, 2002).

Messages and values

The 'conflict' of the topic title implies tensions and confrontations; your analysis should deal with both the conflict represented in the film and the debates raised by the film's subject matter. *It Happened Here*, for example, depicts the fantasy situation of a Nazi invasion of Britain. The events never occurred, yet the conflict between the invading and invaded forces expressed in this historical fantasy reflects very real wartime social fears.

If you choose this topic for your comparative study, you must remember to consider the relationship between the conflicts represented in your films and the social attitudes that they seem to echo. Do the messages and values of the films you have chosen encourage discussion of ideological or social conflicts or do they seem to offer finite conclusions?

You should consider how particular political groups are represented in your films, evaluate the way in which power and authority are represented and analyse how representations of gender, class and ethnicity contribute to the conflicts that arise.

Focus film: *Bloody Sunday*

Bloody Sunday tells the true story of events which occurred in Londonderry on Sunday 30 January 1972. The film adopts a 24-hour time frame in which to relate one version of how 13 people died on that day. Protestant MP Ivan Cooper decides to go ahead with a march against imprisonment without trial. The event took place within the context of IRA terrorism and the counter-attacks of the British forces.

Bloody Sunday takes a stance concerning the run-up to and consequences of this conflict. Your analysis should identify how this stance is constructed through the representation of characters and events. It should also question whether you consider these to be reflective of social attitudes at the time when the events occurred and reflective of social attitudes now. How do the messages and values that you identify affect the viewers of the films? You need to consider whether the particular ideological stance of the film, i.e. that the forces opened fire indiscriminately and without just provocation, offers a true reading of events or just one interpretation.

Comparative films

In the Name of the Father

If your chosen focus film is *Bloody Sunday*, then comparing it with another film that also deals with the Northern Ireland conflict would be appropriate. *In the Name of the Father* (Sheridan, 1993) would be an interesting text for discussion. The film tells the true story of Gerry Conlon, who was imprisoned for being a member of the terrorist group who blew up a Guildford pub in 1974. Beginning in 1970, the film charts the events leading up to the trial and then follows the story of Gerry's fight to clear his name.

The imprisonment of the Guildford Four is represented as a miscarriage of justice. Gerry is represented as an innocent man, wrongly jailed with four others for the attack. Gerry's father, Guiseppe, is also imprisoned as an accomplice to the bombing. The film represents both the police and the judicial system as wilfully overlooking evidence and attempting to assuage public outcry by securing a quick conviction. Gerry Conlon is represented as feckless and irresponsible, but not guilty of the Guildford pub murders. He is seen helping to save a prison guard, after the guard has been set on fire by other inmates. He has petty criminal tendencies, but he is palpably different in his attitudes from the actual IRA members responsible for the bombing.

The jail scenes focus on the relationship between father and son, which at first is full of conflict, but after Guiseppe's death Gerry resolves to continue his father's attempts to clear their name. Sheridan uses the emotive scenes that occur between Guiseppe and Gerry, after their initial lack of closeness has been overcome, in order to secure the viewer's sympathy for the plight of those who have been wrongfully accused.

My Son the Fanatic

My Son the Fanatic (Prasad, 1997) uses a different kind of conflict for the basis of its narrative. Parvez is a Pakistani taxi driver, whose acceptance of Britain brings him into ideological conflict with his son, Farid, an Islamic fundamentalist who is contemptuous of British customs and values. The son brings an Islamic fundamentalist leader into his father's house and plots to rid his city of those elements he sees as wicked and depraved. Parvez is having an affair with a local prostitute, and it is the prostitution in the city that incites the fundamentalists to action. Farid's group is seen attacking the local brothel and it is Parvez who eventually pulls his lover, Betina, out of the conflict.

The conflicts within *My Son the Fanatic* are social as well as ideological. Parvez's family is split apart by his son's desire to cleanse their town. Prasad's film portrays the relationship between Parvez and Betina as mutually supportive and affectionate, whereas the fundamentalist group is undermined by its adoptive leader's desire to stay in Britain (supposedly a place that lacks purity) rather than return to his native country. Parvez's wife moves from a situation of vocality within the household to sitting in the kitchen with the other women while the men talk and make decisions.

Further suggestions

Other films which you could use for discussion include:

- *Dance with a Stranger* (Newell, 1985)
- *Let Him Have It* (Medak, 1991)
- *Some Mother's Son* (George, 1996)
- *Veronica Guerin** (Schumacher, 2003)

Key words

ideological conflict; social conflict; social injustice; social attitudes; gender; class; ethnicity; customs and values

Scottish cinema

This topic asks you to discuss representation in Scottish films. More specifically, you are asked to assess how Scotland and Scottishness are represented in a selection of film texts. The focus films for this topic are *Local Hero* (Forsyth, 1982) and *Orphans** (Mullan, 1997). The exam question will probably not explicitly ask 'How is Scottishness represented in the films you have chosen?', but the focus of your essay should still be how issues of Scottish representation inform the messages and values of your texts.

Make sure that you have notes on the Scottish film industry and how it has influenced the films that have come out of Scotland. Investigate sources of funding for Scottish films and whether or not the Scottish parliament injects money into the film industry. You also need to consider whether Scottish films have been successful in the global marketplace and what people outside Scotland understand about the country from the representations created in Scottish films.

Messages and values

Whichever films you study for this topic, make sure that you discuss the main areas of representation within the texts, the ways in which these representations are created (through characterisation, and micro and macro features) and what kinds of messages and values are implied through these representations.

The representation of Scotland in Hollywood still harks back to the days when Scotland was characterised as a place of myths, and a land that fought to withstand oppression. The romanticisation of Scotland is evident in *Braveheart* (Gibson, 1995)

and *Rob Roy* (Caton-Jones, 1995), which both feature lone heroes fighting for the independence of Scotland. Films produced by the Scottish film industry have more diverse representations. Apply representational areas, such as the family, youth, class and regional identity to your analysis, and discuss in detail what your responses are to the messages and values implied.

Focus film: *Local Hero*

Local Hero tells the story of an American oil company's attempt to buy a Scottish village in order to build an oil refinery on the site. Felix Happer is the head of the oil company. He occupies a detached, godlike position, as is indicated by the celestial *mise-en-scène* of his office. Mac MacIntyre is the 'yuppy' sent to the village to finalise the deal. The film's narrative traces Mac's gradual shift from Houston 'yuppy' to a would-be inhabitant of the village, and ends with Happer designating the village and beach a conservation and research area. *Local Hero* is organised around a series of binary oppositions: industry vs ecology, modernity vs tradition, 'yuppy' individualism vs community values and sentimentality vs practicality.

The film deconstructs clichéd ideas of Scotland as a place of myth and whimsy, through its depiction of the practicality and realism of the village's inhabitants. Mac is attracted to the community spirit evident in the village and by the realistic value systems of the villagers. The attempted 'invasion' of the village by the oil company is not entirely unattractive to the villagers, but the film concludes with a compromise between the villagers' need for financial gain and the awakening of the oil company to a respect for the environment. The Scotland of *Local Hero* is not naive and isolated, but it is a place where an individual's values are reassessed.

Comparative films

Trainspotting*

It is not rural Scotland that is represented in Danny Boyle's 1996 film, but urban Edinburgh. The heroin culture that infiltrated parts of the city in the 1980s is the context for the film's events. Renton, Begbie, Sick Boy and Spud are representatives of the drug-fuelled underclass of the city that exists within its own particular moral world. The schism between the Edinburgh of culture, which is often presented in the media, and the Edinburgh that houses the 'worst toilet in Scotland' is what is presented in this film. According to Renton, 'Scotland is shite', because it is swamped with unemployment and offers the film's protagonists little alternative to crime.

The factors that have contributed to the creation of the underclass that we see in this film should be analysed in any comments you make regarding *Trainspotting**. You will also need to consider how its representation of Scotland compares and contrasts with the very different representation offered in films such as *Local Hero*.

Small Faces

Small Faces (MacKinnon, 1996) is set in Glasgow in the 1960s. The action takes place in the context of a Glasgow populated, and run, by gangs. The narrative follows two

brothers who become caught up in the conflict between two rival gangs. *Small Faces* portrays the violence that can exist within an urban Scottish environment. The Glasgow of the film is a divided place where gang territory is sacred and is only accessible to gang members. The disenfranchised youth of *Trainspotting**, who have no focus apart from drugs, are similar to the young people of *Small Faces*, whose identities are formed by their position within a particular gang.

There are many representational groups in this film which would provide you with useful discussion in your essays. You could look at the way in which young people are presented in the text and discuss the social factors that influence their behaviour. You could compare the representation of urban Scotland in *Small Faces* with that of *Trainspotting**, or discuss the representation of authority figures and consider the role of Malkie Johnson in the local community. You might also compare the representation of the family in this film text with that of other Scottish films.

Ratcatcher

Lynne Ramsay's 1999 film is set on an anonymous Scottish housing estate. The families on the estate suffer from economic hardship and exist within bleak surroundings. *Ratcatcher* is the story of the aftermath of a death. James, a young boy from the estate, allows his friend to die by not saving him from drowning. The rest of the film's narrative follows the consequences of his inaction.

Ratcatcher offers another representation of urban Scotland, which could be compared with the representations offered in *Trainspotting** and *Small Faces*. The film depicts Scottish housing estates as bleak and depressing. The environment in which the children of the film grow up is harsh and uncompromising. What happens to community spirit within this kind of environment and the impact of economic depression on the family would be worthwhile areas of debate.

Further suggestions

You could also include the following films in a comparative study:
- *Shallow Grave** (Boyle, 1994)
- *Young Adam** (Mackenzie, 2003)
- *Morvern Callar* (Ramsay, 2002)
- *Braveheart* (Gibson, 1995)

Key words

Scottishness; global marketplace; urban; rural; romanticisation; family; youth; class; regional identity; binary oppositions; community spirit; heroin culture; underclass; gang rivalry; disenfranchisement; authority figures; economic depression

Comedy

This topic requires you to evaluate how messages and values are communicated through the comedy genre. Comedy is an extremely broad genre and you should remember that the films you choose to study may use comedy in varying ways. You could focus on one of the comedy sub-genres, such as slapstick or satire, in your studies. *The Ladykillers* (Mackendrick, 1955) and *East is East* (O'Donnell, 1999) are the focus films for this topic. Comparative films could perhaps be taken from the Ealing comedies or from a series such as the *Carry On* films.

Messages and values

Analyse both the micro and the macro elements of your films and consider how these contribute to a comic effect, and to messages and values. The cinematography attached to a particular character, for example, can offer information about the status of that character in the film and the way the audience is being invited to respond to that character. The non-diegetic sound used when a particular group of characters is presented on the screen can indicate a serious or comic representation. You might look at the role of groups within the narrative. Are certain characters within your film used as comic relief, to punctuate the more serious scenes? You should consider the ways in which comic conventions, such as the role of the comic foil (the character who is often the butt of the jokes), are used within your films.

The context of your films and the social attitudes that were prevalent at the time are other areas that require analysis. Your teacher may have chosen the *Carry On* series for analysis and the way in which comedy is used to indicate particular attitudes towards gender would be an essential area of debate. You might look at the decades within which the *Carry On* films gained their highest viewing figures and discuss whether or not the attitudes towards gender expressed in these films was truly reflective of dominant social attitudes towards men and women in the 1960s and 1970s. Feminism was becoming prominent in this period and you could evaluate the ways in which feminist discourse responded to the comic depiction of gender roles.

Whichever films you are using to debate how representation is produced within a comic context, you should ensure that you evaluate and challenge the messages and values you identify. Consider how the ideologies that were dominant when the film was made inform representation, but remember to offer your own thoughts on whether the comedy genre is a successful vehicle for messages and values.

Focus film: *East is East*

Set in Salford in 1971, *East is East* focuses on an Asian family living in an otherwise white, working-class community. The film discusses not only the relationship between the Asian family and the white community, but also the relationship between a traditional Asian father and his westernised children. The Khan family is made up of an Asian father (George), a white mother (Ella) and six children. The children provide a cross-section of representations of the position of mixed-race children living in the UK. From the point in the narrative at which the eldest son, Nazir, refuses to go through with an arranged marriage, George attempts to re-establish his position within both his family and community, by arranging other marriages for his children and

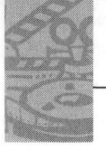

generally becoming more strict. His adherence to the traditions of Pakistan is at odds with the life his wife and family wish to lead in the UK.

The comedy in *East is East* is set against scenes of harrowing family conflict. The film makes serious points about social issues at the same time as offering comic relief. The visit from the Shah family, for example, is comically chaotic, and yet this episode is surrounded by scenes of domestic violence and family alienation. Whether the comedy of this film, and its engagement of the audience, make the messages and values of the film more profound is something that you need to debate in your essay.

Comparative films

Bend it like Beckham

Gurinder Chadha's 2002 study of Asians living in the UK would be a useful partner to *East is East*, as it too considers the position of young Asians in the UK. You could produce an interesting study on the representation of race through a comic filter. Although the parents of the central protagonist in *Bend it Like Beckham* are not as averse to western influences as the father in *East is East*, the children in both films have to battle to follow their own paths. *Bend it Like Beckham* depicts a wide range of Asian characters, including older characters who are highly traditional; young women who are westernised, but still see marriage as their ultimate goal; and a young, gay, Asian man. The film demonstrates the tensions inherent in attempting to preserve an Asian culture and religion within a British context. The comedy is presented via both characterisation and scenarios, for example the three young, fashion-obsessed Asian women who seem to end most of their sentences with 'innit', but the film also makes significant points concerning the ethnically diverse nature of Britain today.

The Full Monty

If your study of comedy includes the depiction of social problems, *The Full Monty* (Cattaneo, 1997) is a suitable text to pair with *East is East*. Both films use a context of social problems to frame the comic elements. *The Full Monty* is set in Sheffield after the decline of the steel industry, and the main protagonists are unemployed men, battling to retain their economic status and dignity in a city suffering severe unemployment.

The Full Monty offers a representation of a marginalised group of men, who each respond to their lack of financial potency in different ways. The film presents the audience with a character who is so ashamed of being unemployed that he cannot tell his wife; a character who might not be able to see his son if he cannot meet alimony payments; and a character who has internalised his lack of self-worth to such an extent that he has lost interest in sex. Cattaneo represents the impact of unemployment comically, through the strip-troupe narrative, but also makes serious points about gender roles and the damage that occurs when a city can no longer support its workforce.

Further suggestions

A discussion of comedy could also include the following films:

- *Four Weddings and a Funeral* (Newell, 1994)
- *Shooting Fish* (Schwartz, 1997)
- *The Most Fertile Man in Ireland* (Appleton, 1999)
- *Waking Ned* (Jones, 1998)

Key words

comic relief; conventions; social attitudes; gender; feminism; family conflict; comic depiction; race; working-class community; sexuality; dominant ideologies; social problems; marginalised group

Section B: the single film close study

How to approach the single film close study

The single film close study element requires you to focus on how messages and values are constructed in one film, rather than a group of films. There are 12 films to choose from:

- *The 39 Steps* (Hitchcock, 1935)
- *The Third Man* (Reed, 1949)
- *Goldfinger* (Hamilton, 1964)
- *The Wicker Man** (Hardy, 1973)
- *Jubilee** (Jarman, 1977)
- *Chariots of Fire* (Hudson, 1981)
- *My Beautiful Laundrette* (Frears, 1987)
- *Secrets and Lies* (Leigh, 1996)
- *House of America* (Evans, 1997)
- *Elizabeth* (Kapur, 1998)
- *Croupier* (Hodges, 1998)
- *Chicken Run* (Lord/Park, 2000)

Although it is possible to link your close-study film with a topic area of your comparative study — for example, *My Beautiful Laundrette* can be linked with passions and repressions — none of the close-study films can be used in section A. Your teacher will probably choose a close study film for you which complements the chosen topic.

Your study can emphasise either the textual or the contextual aspects of your chosen film. If you choose a contextual approach, you could also consider how the film was received, both at the time of its production and by audiences (including yourself) now. The questions in the exam will have either a textual or a contextual focus.

Textual emphasis

You should analyse the micro elements (cinematography, editing, sound and *mise-en-scène*) and the macro elements (genre and narrative) of your chosen film to investigate its messages and values. Your Unit 1 studies will have taught you how particular textual elements can contribute to meaning and generate a response from the viewer, and you should use this knowledge within your Unit 3 exam. The sound elements attached to a particular character might indicate how that character (or the social group to which he or she belongs) is being represented in your focus text. The framing of a character at key points within a film can also help to illustrate the film text's attitude to that character.

Contextual emphasis

Your Unit 2 work on the film industry can also be employed in this part of the exam. The production context of a film might offer you information concerning the way in which a particular film studio is using current social attitudes or dominant ideologies in the creation of the film. You might respond cynically to a film's choice of a particular issue as part of its narrative and decide that the production company or studio is exploiting current social preoccupations. Alternatively, you may decide that the discussion of an issue in your film was useful to social debate. Were there particular attitudes or ideological stances dominant at the time of the film's production? How are these attitudes discussed in the film on which you are focusing?

Reception

A contextual analysis should also include comment on the film's reception, both popular and critical. Collect reviews of your film and consider whether these comment on its messages and values. You could compare critical and popular reception, analysing whether the messages and values of your focus film seem explicit, implicit or not evident to the critics. Don't forget that your own experience of the film is important to your consideration of meanings and ideology. Discuss your own reading of your film's messages and values and consider how your response relates to the others you have collected.

Key words

textual/contextual emphasis; micro elements; macro elements; social attitudes; dominant ideologies; critical reception; popular reception

Case studies

Secrets and Lies

This section ends with case studies on *Secrets and Lies*, *Elizabeth* and *Chicken Run*. These indicate the research you should undertake into your chosen film. Each case study considers the film's contexts, a textual analysis of a sequence from the film, and the messages and values these suggest.

Contexts
Production context

Mike Leigh's *Secrets and Lies* came to cinema screens in 1996. It is a predominantly British film, having a British cast and director, and being produced by two British companies, Channel Four Films and Thin Man Films, as well as CiBy 2000, a French company.

Mike Leigh has had a prolific filmmaking career since his directorial debut in 1971 with *Bleak Moments*. His films for television and the big screen include:

- *Hard Labour* (1973)
- *The Five Minute Films* (1975)
- *Nuts in May* (1976)
- *Kiss of Death* (1977)
- *Who's Who* (1979)
- *Grown-Ups* (1980)
- *Home Sweet Home* (1982)
- *Meantime* (1984)
- *Four Days in July* (1985)
- *The Short and Curlies* (1987)
- *High Hopes* (1988)
- *Life is Sweet* (1990)
- *A Sense of History* (1992)
- *Naked* (1993)
- *Career Girls* (1997)
- *Topsy Turvy* (1999)
- *All or Nothing* (2002)

Leigh's films have received financial backing from both the BBC and Channel Four Films. They are set in Britain and often deal with social problems and individuals who face social deprivation. Leigh's subject matter has included topical issues, such as bulimia (*Life is Sweet*) and the quest to find birth parents (*Secrets and Lies*). His settings are often bleak, working-class areas, where individuals battle with financial instability and unemployment, or households where family life is disintegrating under the pressure of internal struggles. Leigh's characters are not glamorous and they often face real struggles in order to achieve happiness. He is never specific in his identification of the factors that cause his characters' discontent, but the marginalisation of certain groups because of their financial difficulties is a key theme within his films.

Leigh's process of film production is very different from the norm of Hollywood films. His actors are given weeks of rehearsal time in which to create their characters. Often the story of the film is incomplete at the beginning of the rehearsal process and it is through the actors' creation of character that details of the plot are finalised.

Historical and social context

The year of the film's release saw the last year of the Conservative government's lengthy period in office. The focus on individual gain and the privatisation of public services, which had characterised the Tory years, was coming to an end. *Secrets and Lies* depicts two sides of the Tory-governed UK. Cynthia and her daughter Roxanne live in a run-down rented house in a working-class area, while Cynthia's brother Maurice and and his wife Monica have recently bought a brand-new, six-bedroom house in a much more middle-class area. Maurice has his own photographic business,

whereas Roxanne sweeps the streets and Cynthia works in a cardboard box factory. The social and economic divide is obvious, and could be read as a comment on the economic landscape of Britain in 1996.

It is also worth discussing the changes in the adoption law that took place at the time the film was made. Adopted children gained the right to find out who their birth parents were, and this facilitates Hortense's search for Cynthia, her birth mother.

Reception

Secrets and Lies was extremely well received by the critics, and in 1997 was nominated for five Oscars — Best Actress, Best Supporting Actress, Best Director, Best Picture and Best Screenplay. Although it did not win any of these, it was awarded three BAFTAs, for Best Film, Best Actress and Best Screenplay. The British film establishment, as well as British film journalists, saw *Secrets and Lies* as one of the greatest achievements of Leigh's career.

Textual analysis of a sequence: Hortense and Cynthia in the café

This is an important scene in the film, as it is the first conversation that the two characters have about Hortense being Cynthia's daughter. Cynthia initially does not believe that she could be Hortense's mother, but realises during the scene that in fact she is. The scene relates to the film's title in that the secret of Hortense's birth is revealed.

Hortense and Cynthia are shown in a café. The opening shot positions the pair to the left of the frame. The women sit on the same side of the table, with Cynthia seated between Hortense and the wall. She appears trapped by the setting and also by the conversation she is having. The regimented seating around them is empty and no waiting staff can be seen. The viewer is therefore allowed to concentrate on the conversation between the two with no other visual distraction, and the isolation of the pair indicates not only their individual lonely states, but also their isolation with their now shared secret. The women's positions at the table, side by side rather than opposite each other, allow them to occupy separate halves of the same frame. Their connection and their distance at this point in the narrative is thus indicated.

The two characters are dressed very differently. Hortense wears a black suit, which reflects her mourning, and Cynthia dresses in much lighter and probably cheaper clothes. Their economic and social status is reflected in this aspect of *mise-en-scène*, and Cynthia herself comments on their difference.

There is only one transition in the whole of the scene and this is from the opening shot of Hortense and Cynthia to the left of the frame, to the pair framed symmetrically in mid shot from the opposite side of the café table. The camera's movement makes the scene become more intimate and allows the viewer to see the women's expressions more clearly. The camera remains static within this second section of the scene and positions the viewer as if he or she were seated on the other side of the table, listening to the conversation.

The body language apparent within this scene is important to the expression of meaning. Hortense seems less anxious than Cynthia, who fidgets with her cigarette and looks away towards the wall when she expresses her 'shame' at not immediately knowing who Hortense's father was. Hortense does not cry, but asks questions concerning the circumstances of her birth. She appears almost numb, in contrast to Cynthia's fits of crying.

This sequence illustrates many of the core pre-occupations of the film. The representations of family and social class are discussed by the scene's *mise-en-scène*, as well as its dialogue. The conversation between the pair concerning jobs only serves to make their economic status apparent and the framing of this conversation allows the audience to understand the tensions, expectations, disappointments and problematic dynamics that exist within the families of this film.

Messages and values

The family

The stereotypical representation of the nuclear family, comprising mother, father and two children, is absent from *Secrets and Lies*. In this film, families are characterised by absence, and the secrets and lies of the film's title refer to these absences. The missing elements provide reasons for the characters' unhappiness — Monica and Maurice lack a child, Hortense lacks parents and Cynthia lacks a man in her life. Family is at once supportive and destructive in this film, and Leigh offers us an image of family that is complex and chaotic, but ultimately soothing. You need to evaluate whether or not this representation of the family reflects the social norm in the latter years of the twentieth century.

The opening sequence of the film shows Hortense at her adoptive mother's funeral. Her father is already dead and she is left with only her adoptive brothers, who seem more concerned with arguing over who will live in their dead mother's house than grieving. Hortense's subsequent search for Cynthia, her birth mother, creates the momentum and tensions of the film. She is accepted by Cynthia, and accompanies her to Roxanne's 21st-birthday party. However, it is at this event that the secrets and lies of the characters' lives are exposed. The absence of family which Hortense experiences after the death of her adoptive mother acts as her motivation and eventually, after her identity has been revealed to Maurice, Monica and Roxanne, she gains some resolution to her quest. The last scene of the film shows Hortense and Roxanne chatting in Cynthia's garden, implying that trust has been restored and that Hortense may finally have found a family.

Absence is also a key feature of Maurice and Monica's marriage. They are childless and it is revealed that Monica is unable to have children. This provides the root of Monica's resentment of Cynthia, who has had two unplanned children, one of whom she gave up for adoption. 'You can't miss what you never had,' states Monica in relation to sibling relationships, but Maurice's response to this statement proves that the child they cannot have is sorely missed.

The relationship between siblings is a fertile area of analysis, too. While Hortense and Roxanne seem to be moving towards a positive sibling relationship, Hortense's adoptive brothers appear only as individuals squabbling over their dead mother's house. They are absent from the narrative after this point and are not shown offering any support for Hortense in her search for her birth mother. Monica has not seen her brother Craig for a long while, but expresses no loss at his living in Saudi Arabia. The relationship between Maurice and Cynthia is complex and it is evident from their discussions that Maurice, as a 17-year-old, acted as a surrogate father to Roxanne. Cynthia's dependence on Maurice is thus part of the characters' back stories, and in the film, Cynthia responds to Maurice as both brother, father figure and even, at times, absentee partner.

Parents and children are also represented as having complex relationships. Cynthia and Roxanne clash as Cynthia takes an almost prurient interest in her daughter's love life. There is an implication that Cynthia desires both to live her life through her daughter, but also to guide Roxanne away from making the same mistakes that she made. The dialogue between Roxanne and Cynthia is mostly confrontational, and this is only softened after the secrets and lies of the mother's life are revealed.

Social class

Secrets and Lies represents the class divide through the different lifestyles of Cynthia and Maurice. Cynthia and Roxanne live in the house where Cynthia and Maurice grew up, and Cynthia's lack of hope for her own future is reflected by the fact that the house has remained the same since she was a child. The *mise-en-scène* of the house is characterised by drabness and decay. It is terraced and located in a working-class area of the city. It still has an outside toilet and lacks any sign of modernisation. Maurice and Cynthia's father's room remains as he left it, crammed with the dusty clothes and possessions of the dead man. The room represents the stasis that characterises Cynthia's life. She has neither the money nor the motivation to update her house, and it is Maurice who offers to pay for the damp to be examined. Her clothes are either old or inappropriate for a woman of her age and she attempts to cling onto her perception of herself as an attractive female by pointing out her 'nice legs' to her daughter. Roxanne and Cynthia work in manual, low-paid jobs, with no hope of improving their living circumstances because of their economic situation.

In contrast, Monica and Maurice live in a clean, light and modern six-bedroom house on a middle-class housing estate. Their house is pristine and reflects Monica's need to convert her unhappiness into activity. Monica is seen stencilling patterns onto furniture and hoovering in an attempt to divert her attention from the child that she cannot have. Maurice is a successful photographer with his own business and Monica does not work. In Cynthia's eyes, Monica is privileged and snobbish, although she comes to understand why Monica might need diversionary pursuits. The *mise-en-scène* of Monica and Maurice's house represents many aspects of their lives. Everything in the house is bright and new, indicating their distance from the working-class concerns of Cynthia and Roxanne. But its cleanliness is also clinical and lifeless. The absence of warmth reflects the tensions between the couple and their childless status.

The two homes in *Secrets and Lies* represent the different ends of the economic spectrum. Maurice has moved on from his working-class roots, but Cynthia is still embedded in the world and class of her childhood. The social world of this film seems to reflect the division of wealth apparent in any city in Britain. You need to evaluate whether or not you think Mike Leigh is making any political point through the economic divisions and class divides represented in this film.

Race

The representation of Hortense breaks away from the stereotype of a marginalised black individual. Her race is not the focus of the narrative, and Cynthia's shock at having a black daughter seems to be based more on the fact that she could not remember sleeping with a black man and had not been shown the baby after its birth, than on any racial prejudice.

Hortense is an optometrist, a profession for which a degree-level education is necessary. She lives alone in a modern, clean and well-designed flat. We do not know whether she owns or rents the flat, but the *mise-en-scène* implies a solid financial situation. Hortense's adoptive mother's house is also large and well maintained. There does not seem to have been any shortage of money or affection in Hortense's upbringing, and she enters the film as an independent, well-spoken, young woman. The black community pays its respects at Hortense's adoptive mother's funeral and, at least in this context, it seems to be supportive of Hortense. She also appears in a scene with a friend, who offers her support while she is grieving. Significantly, the two women have a conversation about the value of honest conversations with parents, in which Hortense expresses her regret at not having asked her adoptive mother more questions and her friend expresses her desire to have her life kept secret from her mother.

The representation of Hortense as a successful, professional, supported, middle-class, black woman is entirely different from the representation of her birth mother Cynthia, as a working-class woman trapped by both her own hopelessness and her lack of financial stability. Hortense's presence in the narrative, along with the images of the black community we are offered, reflect the multiracial nature of British cities.

Key words

working class; unemployment; internal struggle; marginalisation; middle class; family; absence; social class; race

Elizabeth

Contexts

Production context

Elizabeth was directed by Shekhar Kapur in 1998. The production companies behind the film were Channel Four Films and Working Title Films, from the UK, and Polygram Filmed Entertainment, a US company. The production context of *Elizabeth* is, therefore, predominantly British. Although *Elizabeth* is essentially a costume drama, it uses

the conventions of a thriller, such as labyrinthine plots and conspiracies, in order to engage the viewer. Kapur's filmography includes *Bandit Queen** (1994) and *The Four Feathers* (2002).

Historical and social context

The film is set in the sixteenth century and depicts the events that led to the establishment of Elizabeth I as the 'Virgin Queen'. Regardless of the distance between the time in which the film was set and the time in which it was made, there are some interesting parallels that can be drawn. *Elizabeth* begins with the slaughter of individuals because of their religious beliefs. The prejudices and intolerance evoked in these initial scenes still exist in the twenty-first century — the purging of individuals whose beliefs do not conform to the dominant ideological position within a country still occurs today. The political intrigues of the court and the power-mongering of individuals within politics are also aspects that the viewer can recognise as still existing today.

Reception

Elizabeth received praise from both academic and popular critics. The film received seven Oscar nominations and won one, for Best Makeup. Fans of the film were disappointed with the lack of Oscars, but were much happier with the response of the British film establishment at the BAFTA awards. *Elizabeth* won six BAFTAs, including Best Actress for Cate Blanchett and Best Supporting Actor for Geoffrey Rush.

Textual analysis of a sequence: the film's opening

The opening sequence of *Elizabeth* introduces the viewer to the film's time, place and themes. It is 1554 and Mary I, a devout Catholic, is on the throne. The film opens with the non-diegetic soundtrack of a sixteenth-century-style piece of music. The notes are elongated and the vocals rise to a pitch during the opening sequence. The soundtrack not only evokes the period in which the film is set, but also the fervour of religious feeling at that time. The opening credit sequence is saturated with the colour red and the viewer cannot help but feel that both passion and death will play a major part in this film. The crosses that are seen in the opening credit sequence also highlight the connection between religion, passion and death.

The cinematography in this sequence emphasises the plight of the condemned Protestant prisoners. The opening credits cut to medium shots of the Protestants having their hair cut off, in preparation for their execution. The viewer is presented with overhead shots that give a clear view of the brutal way in which the guards are cutting the prisoners' hair. A close-up of the knife used to cut the prisoner's hair and the blood from their heads on the knife is then used to emphasise the barbaric treatment still further.

As the prisoners are made to walk to their deaths, the camera takes an overhead position in order to make the viewer feel as if he or she is one of the onlookers within the scene. In common with many of the other members of the crowd, our sympathies are encouraged to rest with the Protestants. The camera then cuts to an overhead shot of the prisoners standing in the middle of piles of sticks, waiting for their deaths. They appear small, vulnerable and trapped. They are at the centre of the frame, surrounded by wood, crowds and officials from the Catholic church. The film cuts to a mid shot of the men and woman on the bonfire. The viewer is presented with their terrified expressions and with the emotion on the crowd's faces around them. The crowd and the prisoners fill the frame and we are given the impression of an increasingly fraught and chaotic situation. The onlookers attempt to help the prisoners die quickly by adding wood to the bonfire and the frame is full of those who do not wish to see these prisoners die for their beliefs. The medium shot of flames leaping, while the Catholic bishop is pictured through the flames, standing rigid and emotionless, indicates the chasm between the two religious groups. As the sequence comes to an end, the frame begins to fill with flames. The non-diegetic sound rises to a jarring climax and the Protestant prisoners are seen dying.

Criticism of the oppression of those who articulate different beliefs and the prejudice surrounding this oppression is a key message within this opening sequence. Power is also a key theme in *Elizabeth* and this sequence indicates this clearly.

Messages and values
Power
Elizabeth offers an interesting deconstruction of the impact of power both on the state and on the individual. Mary I, the devout Catholic who reigns at the beginning of the film, uses her position as the monarch to purge England of Protestantism. The opening sequence shows how the individual stance of the monarch, if translated into political action, can have devastating consequences.

When Princess Elizabeth becomes queen, the power seems to rest (initially at least) behind the throne. For the first section of the film, she is little more than a figurehead. She is young and inexperienced, using the statesmen to inform her decisions. The young Elizabeth is a pawn in the English court, her power muted by the dominance of the (often calculating) men around her. The Duke of Norfolk is a key player in the conspiracies designed to take power away from Elizabeth. She may live in luxury, but she has little real political power.

The scenes in which Elizabeth transforms from young ingénue to the Virgin Queen recognisable from portraits represent a transformation from individual to head of state. Elizabeth takes control of the political landscape of England and one of her first actions is a bloody overthrow of the forces against the crown. Elizabeth's advisers attempt to persuade her to marry a European monarch to secure England's position, but she rejects their efforts. The costume of the Virgin Queen is restrictive and negates her gender, perhaps an indication that power comes at a price. Elizabeth has to subsume her hopes of love and individual freedom in order to prove herself a force to be reckoned with.

Gender

As a dramatised re-creation of a queen's ascent to the throne and subsequent dominance over her country, *Elizabeth* is primarily the story of a woman. The film considers the position of women in the sixteenth century through both the narrative and the micro features of the film.

The position of women at this time was secondary to men. Neither Mary nor Elizabeth would have been monarchs if there had been a male alternative. Elizabeth has to contend with the preconceptions that both court and country have of women. She is surrounded by male advisers who, with one exception, deem her incapable of making state-related decisions. Elizabeth is deemed to be less potent as a monarch because she is female, and is encouraged to marry in order to secure her position abroad. Elizabeth has to strip herself of many of her female interests and desires in order to secure the confidence of the court and the country. Symbolically, the highly restrictive Virgin Queen costume she adopts, with its white face and high hairline, indicates what Elizabeth has given up in order to rule England.

Traditional gender roles are not fixed in this film. *Elizabeth* ultimately places power in the hands of its central female character. This challenge to gender roles has its ultimate example in the scene in which Elizabeth finds Anjou (the French prince proposed as her husband) cavorting in female clothes.

Although attitudes to gender have changed since the sixteenth century, the film reflects current debates concerning women in politics, and the strategies that female politicians today are forced to use in order to secure respect. Contemporary female politicians may not have to whiten their faces, but if Margaret Thatcher is any indication, a lowering of the voice and harshening of manner (both suggesting de-feminisation) might be the twentieth-century equivalent.

Key words

religion; oppression; prejudice; intolerance; passion; death; power; politics; gender; preconceptions; de-feminisation

Chicken Run

Contexts

Production context

Chicken Run (2000) was written and directed by Peter Lord and Nick Park. It is an example of stop-motion animation, a time-consuming process in which models are moved fractionally and then shot. The thousands of individual shots are then linked to approximate movement. The film was produced by Aardman Animations and Pathé Pictures Ltd from the UK, and Dreamworks SKG from the US. Aardman Animations is the company set up by Nick Park and his team, and its involvement in production ensured a good degree of artistic freedom for the filmmakers. Dreamworks SKG is the company founded and run by Steven Spielberg. Although *Chicken Run* did have some American backing, it is predominantly a British product. The Aardman Animations team has produced a number of financially and critically successful animated films, including *Creature Comforts* (1990), *Wallace and Gromit: A Grand Day Out* (1992), *Wallace and Gromit: The Wrong Trousers* (1993) and *Wallace and Gromit: A Close Shave* (1995).

Historical and social context

In the late twentieth century, computer generated imagery (CGI) had become familiar to cinema audiences through films such as *Toy Story* (Lasseter, 1995) and *Shrek* (Adamson, 2001) and it is testament to the characterisation and expressiveness of the stop-motion technique that within this CGI-saturated context, *Chicken Run* was such a success. The film is based loosely on the narrative of John Sturges' 1962 film *The Great Escape*, and as such proved popular with adults who had seen the 'original', as well as with animation lovers and children. The themes of entrapment and escape are universal and this made the film accessible to a wide viewing public.

Reception

Chicken Run was nominated for many awards and won a significant number. It received the 2001 Blockbuster Entertainment award for Favourite Family Film, the 2001 Broadcast Film Critics Association Award for Best Animated Film, the 2001 Motion Picture Sound Editors award for Best Sound Editing in an Animated Film and the 2000 New York Film Critics Circle award for Best Animated Film. *Chicken Run* took $17 500 000 in its opening weekend in America and £3 850 000 in its opening weekend in the UK, proving it to be both financially and critically successful.

Textual analysis of a sequence: the film's opening

The opening sequence of *Chicken Run* indicates the intertextuality of the film. The sequence presents one of Ginger's failed attempts to escape and her subsequent imprisonment in the coal bin. This echoes Steve McQueen's 'cooler king' character's escape attempts in *The Great Escape*.

The non-diegetic soundtrack that accompanies the opening credits creates an atmosphere of adventure and excitement. The viewer is immediately introduced to a narrative that promises scenes of high tension and drama. The opening shot of the film is of the moon. The camera then pans down to frame the chicken run through the fence that imprisons the hens. The setting of the film is thus established as a prison. The camera then continues to pan away from the fence, eventually resting with a low angle shot of the approaching Mr Tweedy, with one of his dogs. He is presented as threatening and the close-up shot that follows, as he checks the padlock on the gate to the chicken run, seals his representation as jailer of the hens. The sequence then cuts to a shot of Ginger hiding in the shadows. The *mise-en-scène* establishes a sense of danger and risk — Ginger might be using the shadows to hide, but the darkness also holds the dogs and the farmer. The sequence cuts back to a shot of Mr Tweedy circling the perimeter fence. This shot also contains the lookout tower, which is at the edge of the fence, another image that resembles a prisoner of war camp.

Mr Tweedy is shot in fragments for the first few minutes of the film. We see his hand, his boots and shadowed sections of his face. This is a device usually associated with those characters in films that have malevolent intent, and it confirms Mr Tweedy's negative representation. The transitions used in this sequence are cuts and these speed up as the tension of the situation mounts. After the hen gets stuck under the fence and the escape plan begins to founder, the fast cutting creates tension. Ginger attempts to flee from the dogs and Mr Tweedy, eventually running up the steps towards the farmer's house. She is framed in front of the door, trapped between it and the dogs. The music is fast-paced and builds to a pitch of tension when the dogs move to strike. At this point in the sequence, however, the pace changes. The front door opens and the non-diegetic sound quietens. The dogs are seen cowering, Ginger's terrified eyes are shown in close-up and the camera begins to pan up the body of Mrs Tweedy. The low angle and upward pan present Mrs Tweedy as powerful. The light source is behind her and she appears to stand out as the authority figure in the scene (and indeed the film). Ginger is thrown into the 'cooler' and one of the last shots of the sequence is a point-of-view shot of Mr Tweedy's angry face as he closes the door on her. The sequence then cuts to another point-of-view shot from the hens inside the chicken run, as they watch the angry face of Mr Tweedy loom threateningly.

The opening sequence establishes the pattern of representation that is explored in the rest of the film. Authority and gender roles are presented in this sequence via the cinematography, editing, sound and *mise-en-scène*. The intertextual elements of *Chicken Run* are highlighted from the outset and the viewer is introduced immediately to the themes of incarceration and escape.

Messages and values

Gender

The characters in the film are predominantly female. The female characters in *Chicken Run* provide the majority of the motivation for action in this film, either in attempts to escape or attempts to turn the chickens into pies.

The chickens represent a cross-section of female types. Ginger, for example, is independent, free-thinking and not easily seduced by the 'charm' of the American rooster Rocky.

The chickens' sole function is egg production, and they are prized only for their ability to conform to this purpose. This reduction of the gender characteristics of the chickens to a single function — that of producing eggs — can be read as analogous to the position of women in the 1940s and 1950s, when feminism was not a common discourse and women were often perceived as merely homemakers. Although Ginger craves the freedom to be able to choose which path she follows in life, many of the other chickens are resigned to their role. It is only when Edwina is slaughtered at the beginning of the film, because of her lack of productivity, that the chickens begin to question their position.

The character of Mrs Tweedy, however, breaks with stereotype in a violent manner. She controls the relationship between herself and Mr Tweedy and makes the decision that the farm should move towards pie production. She is ruthless, uncompromising and brutal, and is the only character that strikes fear into all of the other characters, including the two guard dogs. Mrs Tweedy's gender has been subsumed by her focused desire for profit.

The main male characters in *Chicken Run* are Mr Tweedy, Rocky, Fowler, Fetcher and Nick. The rats occupy the position of wartime spivs and contribute to the film's gender discussions by simply observing the hens' plight, rather than helping them. Mr Tweedy is dominated by his wife and is constantly chastised for his ineptitude and lack of vision. Rocky is brash, often lazy and needs female adulation to preserve his sense of being a potent creature. It is Ginger's grit and determination that eventually cause Rocky to return to the chicken run to aid the escape, and Ginger who precipitates Rocky's revision of his attitude towards females. Fowler exists through his air-force past, attempting to take control of the chicken run and organise the hens. His inability to do this effectively is also typical of the other male characters. All three assume that their role should be authoritative and none of them has the strength of character to occupy this role. The gender discussions in *Chicken Run* are not overt, and neither are they the focus of the text, but they do highlight issues of gender roles and assumptions about gender that are still current.

Nationality

The inhabitants of the chicken run are predominantly English, with Mac as the Scottish character. The film's parallel with *The Great Escape* would make Mr and Mrs Tweedy the German guards. The oppressed in this film are therefore the allied forces, with Rocky providing the US contingent. Rocky articulates a stereotypical view of America, dubbing it 'the land of the free and the home of the brave' — an ironic statement considering that Rocky has deceived the chickens by continuing their belief that he can fly and has himself been imprisoned in a circus, probably never having really experienced the 'freedom' of America.

Through its characterisation, the film prompts us to debate stereotypes of nationality, such as the stiff upper lip of the English Fowler and the classless, gung-ho attitude of the American Rocky.

Authority

Authority for the hens is the couple that have imprisoned them. The cinematography, sound and *mise-en-scène* attached to Mrs Tweedy at the beginning of the film highlight her authoritative position. The first shot of her is from a low angle and for most of the film she is shot in this position of dominance. Her hair is scraped back into a tight bun and she walks with military bearing. The non-diegetic soundtrack that provides a backdrop to Mrs Tweedy's entrance into scenes is ominous, relentless and predatory in tone. Her position remains dominant until she is cut free from the plane and then trapped by the very machinery she wanted to use to make her pies.

The chickens have a dual response to authority, however. On one hand, they fight to escape from the Tweedy's oppression and are dismissive of Fowler's attempts to enforce order in the camp. On the other hand, the majority of the hens are happy to relinquish control of their escape to Rocky. They are desperate to believe in his flying skills, despite Mac's calculations concerning the ability of chickens to fly and Ginger's sceptical attitude towards Rocky's organisation of their flying lessons.

Those who are desperate can be exploited, and this idea is articulated in the film through the hens' belief in Rocky. In one scene he is seen issuing instructions from a bath, while being given a massage by two hens. It is only Ginger who seems to realise that this situation is ridiculous.

Authority is represented as necessary in the film. It is not the authority over others that is applauded, however, but the ability to take control of one's own life and have authority over one's future.

Key words

stop-motion animation; computer-generated imagery (CGI); artistic freedom; entrapment; escape; intertextuality; gender; nationality; authority

Questions
&
Answers

This section of the guide contains six questions typical of **Unit FS3: Messages and Values**. There are four questions from section A of the exam and two from section B. For each question two answers are provided — one of A-grade standard and one of C-grade standard. It is important that you use these answers as a structure and content guide rather than as model answers. You may choose to answer the same questions differently, using other examples, and achieve equally good marks. Consider the language used in the answers and the way in which the material is organised and the arguments are structured. These elements will be of most use to you when you are preparing for the exam.

Examiner's comments

Each of the candidate answers is accompanied by examiner's comments, both within the essay itself and at the end of the answer. These are preceded by the icon *e* and indicate where credit is due. In the weaker answers, they also point out areas for improvement. Pay particular attention to the skills highlighted in the examiner's comments and the problems identified. The comments should help you in your preparation for the exam.

Section A: Swinging Britain, 1963–73

How are the lives of young people in the period 1963–73 represented in the films you have studied?

Grade-A answer

There is a diversity of representations of young people during the 10-year period of this topic. However, a consistency across the films I have studied is the representation of youth as being to some extent rebellious. The films I will use in this essay are *A Hard Day's Night* (Lester, 1964) and *A Clockwork Orange** (Kubrick, 1971).

   A Hard Day's Night is essentially a promotional film for the Beatles. Its target audience was the young fans of the band and those young people who might become fans. The majority of the Beatles's fans at the time were young teenage girls, and because of this Richard Lester had to make sure that the band members were represented as fun-loving, available and, to some degree, anarchic, but not too dangerous as to alienate their audience. The Beatles are seen in many scenes of mayhem and fun. They are chased through the streets of London and fool around on a playing field. The band members are represented as accessible. They have an anti-authoritarian manner that their target audience would have related to, but they are not seen in situations which would have alienated their young female audience, such as sexual scenarios or situations involving drink and drugs. Ultimately, the representation of youth in *A Hard Day's Night* is exciting, but safe.

> 📝 The candidate identifies the text's purpose well and gives a clear explanation of how this informs representation.

The band's anti-authoritarian stance can be seen in the dealings with the management. They have a different set of priorities from those who are trying to keep them on the straight and narrow. The Beatles tease their manager and their disappearance at key points causes much concern. However, the young men do ultimately perform when they should. The social fear of rebellious youth that was prevalent in the 1960s is suggested by this film, but the Beatles are more madcap than dangerously anarchic.

   John Lennon's grandfather represents age in this text and he avoids stereotypical representation. He is the cause of many of the real problems and potential crises within the film and is utterly irresponsible and selfish. Next to this character, the Beatles's behaviour is diluted and does not appear so problematic. It is as if the film relocates social fears about irresponsibility into age, rather then youth.

   Stanley Kubrick's *A Clockwork Orange** is a very different type of film. It asks the viewer to consider which is worse: the behaviour of Alex and his 'droogs' or that of the authority figures who 'treat' Alex. Unlike that seen in *A Hard Day's Night*, Alex's behaviour is extremely antisocial. He is both a rapist and a murderer, taking every opportunity to work against what he sees as the mundane existence of his parents' generation. Alex and his 'droogs' have set up an alternative social group to combat what they see as an alien world. They have their own hierarchy, language and rules.

question

During the first part of the film the behaviour of the 'droogs' is appalling, and you would expect the viewer to have no sympathy at all for Alex. The voiceover for the film, however, is Alex's, and he acts as our narrative guide, often giving articulate justification for his actions. The viewer is therefore thrown into some confusion as to how to respond to this particular representation of youth.

However, the authority figures in A Clockwork Orange* (doctors, prison officers, social workers, parents and politicians) are represented negatively too. Alex is subjected to a hideous aversion therapy and is treated by the doctors as a laboratory experiment rather than a human being. He is dehumanised, degraded, used as a political pawn and abused in the name of politics and science.

What is challenging about Kubrick's film is that none of the characters is particularly attractive. The young characters are violent and so are the older ones. The film seems to suggest that without responsibility, violent and anarchic behaviour can occur, but even given responsibility, these negative situations can arise anyway.

> 🖉 This is an excellent consideration of audience reception. The candidate speculates effectively on the impact of the messages and values of the film on the audience.

A Hard Day's Night represents carefree youth. The young people of the film have freedom and excitement. The promotional aspects of the film aim to represent the Beatles and their fans as young, free, moderately irresponsible, but ultimately unthreatening. A Clockwork Orange*, on the other hand, offers a representation of what can happen to young people placed in a situation of institutional violence. These films seem to exist at almost opposite ends of the spectrum. One aims to please its youthful audience, at the same time as not offending the establishment. The other offers a very complex comment on how youth can be made violent in particular social situations.

> 🖉 This is an excellent response to the question, which uses appropriate textual examples to substantiate its points. Both films are discussed with confidence and the messages and values of each are explored in detail. The issue of social context and its impact on film content is explored, as are the aims of the films themselves. There is a clear sense of an individual voice in this essay and the candidate has obviously considered both films in a thorough and intelligent way.

■ ■ ■

Grade-C answer

Young people are represented in many different ways in the films I studied for this topic. The representations range from fun to rebellious. The films I am going to focus on for this answer are A Hard Day's Night (Richard Lester, 1964) and If... (Lindsay Anderson, 1968).

A Hard Day's Night is the story of the Beatles trying to get to gigs. The Beatles have a group of managers who try to look after them, but they get into lots of situations that mean that they might not get to their gig. They are rebellious and try to avoid being told what to do by those characters who are older than them. The Beatles' managers are often seen despairing of their clients.

All four members of the band get into scrapes and spend much of their time playing around. They are represented as young and carefree, which is illustrated by the scene in which they run around on a playing field. They are seen on a train with a man who obviously believes in the class system. This scene shows that the Beatles are represented as not believing in the same class system as those around them.

> 🖉 These comments need to have more specific contextual substantiation. They seem rather literal.

The film has a soundtrack of the Beatles's own music. The pop music of the 1960s is represented as being fun and light. The lyrics in the songs do not talk about depression, drugs or any other negative subjects, but are about love and having a good time. This adds to the representation of youth in this film as a group of people who have few responsibilities and should be allowed to live freely.

If... is a very different film. Anderson seems to be much more negative about the young people he represents. The boys in the school in *If...* are often arrogant and even have violent tendencies. Perhaps because this film was made later than *A Hard Day's Night*, the fun and lightness of the early 1960s did not really exist any more. Viewers watching *If...* would be concerned about the behaviour of the boys in the school and might see this as a product of the times.

> 🖉 The candidate does not engage with the ideological background to this film and makes unsubstantiated assumptions concerning viewer response.

The films I have studied make different points about the lives of young people. I think *A Hard Day's Night* is a picture of a time when everything was free and easy and life was 'swinging'. *If...*, on the other hand, creates a much more disturbing picture of young people.

> 🖉 The candidate shows a good understanding of the films studied. There is some attempt to engage with the importance of social and historical contexts as influences on representation. However, many of the points are rather literal and there are some particularly simplistic points made about the attitudes of the 1960s. There is also an assumption in this essay that representation is one-dimensional and that a discussion of representation ends with contemplation of what the director intended. The section on *If...* is cursory and does not use textual features to substantiate points.

Section A: Passions and repressions

What messages and values influence characters' behaviour in the films you have studied? You may wish to refer to one key character from each film.

Grade-A answer

The historical context of a film, either the time in which the film was made or the time in which it is set, is extremely important when considering its messages and values. In this essay, I am going to consider the characters of Laura from *Brief Encounter* (Lean, 1945) and Stevens from *The Remains of the Day* (Ivory, 1993) in my discussion of the influence of messages and values.

Brief Encounter was made in 1945 and to some degree aimed to reinvigorate the British cinema public after the hardships of the Second World War. It deals with the romance between Laura and Alec. One key feature of the film is that at the end of the narrative, the characters agree to end their romance and return to their partners. Laura adheres to the dominant view of women in the 1940s. She is a married woman who is unable to break out of her relationship to reach for something more exciting. Her voice-over for the film is guilt-ridden and full of her feelings of responsibility towards her family. She is able to flirt with the idea of a romance, but is unable to realise her feelings fully because ultimately she conforms to what is expected of her. She does not challenge the stereotypes of the time by walking away from her commitments, but offers an image of emotional infidelity.

In the postwar context of *Brief Encounter*, the viewing public wanted a mixture of excitement and safety. The turbulence of the war years had caused unrest and economic hardship, and what the viewing public wanted most was escapism. This escapism could not be too radical, however; *Brief Encounter* uses the potential escapism of a romance, but tempers it by making the encounter short and non-physical. Through the character of Laura, the film articulates both passion and repression. She might dream of escape with Alec, but in order to preserve her (and the audience's) sense of social values, the escape is kept as a dream.

> ☑ This is a sound discussion of how historical context and viewer expectations can inform characterisation and representation.

The Remains of the Day is set prior to the beginning of the Second World War. Stevens works as head butler in a stately home and runs his household like a military operation. His devotion to his employer indicates his attitude to the class divide. He has absolute belief in the opinion of those who occupy a higher social position than himself. Stevens is utterly respectful of his master and does not question his beliefs. Even after his employer has been disgraced as a Nazi sympathiser, Stevens refuses to admit that his master knowingly became involved with right-wing politics. The film suggests that it is as much the working classes as their masters who can be responsible for perpetuating the class divide.

📝 The candidate makes an interesting challenge to the traditional notion that it is the ruling classes who fix and perpetuate the class system.

Stevens is a character ruled by repression. He represses his judgements of his employer and also any romantic leanings he might have. The housekeeper, Miss Kenton, attempts to liberate Stevens's romantic nature — this happens in a key scene, in which she catches him reading a romantic novel. She approaches him, but he retreats to the corner of the room. He is immobilised by her feelings for him and acts defensively. At the end of the film's narrative, the viewer understands Stevens's regret at this lost chance of love, yet when romance is available he shies away. *The Remains of the Day* offers a picture of how the class system and those who believe in it unquestioningly are ultimately repressed and repressive.

Both of the films I have chosen to study offer comments on how the social values of a particular time can affect an individual's behaviour. Both Laura and Stevens are unable to break free of what they consider to be their social responsibility and in the end are left feeling alone and unsatisfied.

📝 This is a very articulate response to the question. The candidate begins by offering an interesting thesis and then argues the case systematically, using well-chosen texts and examples. There is good evidence of both textual and contextual understanding. The essay avoids becoming merely a character study, and offers intelligent points concerning the impact of dominant social attitudes on both characters and film texts. Messages and values are explored with a high degree of understanding and with a confident, individual voice.

■ ■ ■

Grade-C answer

There are many factors that can influence a character's behaviour in a film. One could be the behaviour of other characters and a second might be how an individual character sees him or herself. For this essay, I will concentrate on the central characters in *Brief Encounter* (David Lean, 1945) and *My Beautiful Laundrette* (Stephen Frears, 1985).

In *Brief Encounter*, the central character, Laura, is married, but she begins a relationship with a married man, Alec. The relationship is not sexual and is only 'brief', but it is one that changes Laura's life. The film was made just after the Second World War and Laura is a woman who is stereotyped by the attitudes of the time. She speaks with a perfect accent, feels guilty about her feelings for Alec and eventually goes back to her husband. Leaving her husband would not have been an option for a woman like Laura in 1945. David Lean's film suggests that affairs are wrong. The romantic feelings of Laura and Alec towards each other are strong and yet he does not let their relationship blossom. Instead the viewer sees the pair say goodbye to each other at the end of the film.

e There is too much character description here. The candidate needs to consider what has influenced this representation.

My Beautiful Laundrette is a film made in the 1980s, when attitudes towards relationships were very different. If Laura and Alec had lived in this period, they would probably have left their families and had a full relationship. *My Beautiful Laundrette* tells the story of a young Asian man who runs a laundrette and the ex-Nazi white man he employs there. The two men become closer throughout the film and eventually begin a homosexual relationship. They have to keep their relationship hidden for two reasons. First, many people at the time the film was made were still intolerant of homosexuality. Second, one of the men is white and one is Asian. Their relationship is therefore of mixed race and this would also be seen as unacceptable by many people in the 1980s.

e This paragraph is not specific enough. What are the names of the two young men? Where do they live and does this have an impact on representation?

Although the two films I have studied were made over 40 years apart, they both tell stories of repression. All of the central characters have to repress their true feelings in order to conform to public opinion.

e The candidate has selected two interesting texts to compare and shows some understanding of these chosen films. There is also some identification of how the messages and values of the times in which the films were made can influence representation. The essay lacks specificity, however, and needs to include much more actual textual detail in the discussion. Certain assumptions are made about the dominant social attitudes of the times in which the films were produced, which render some of the comments far too simplistic. There is an assumption in the answer that little has changed since the 1940s regarding attitudes towards homosexuality. A cinematically literate audience or, indeed, any audience would have had some exposure to cinema with homosexual under/overtones.

Section A: Scottish cinema

Discuss the representation of community in the films you have studied for this topic.

Grade-A answer

The representation of community is a significant feature in the films I have studied for this topic. The traditional preconceptions of a community as a mutually supportive social unit are present, yet often this traditional notion is deconstructed. The representation of community is used in my chosen group of films to indicate wider debates concerning economic status and personal identity.

> The candidate offers a clear, well-presented thesis in the introduction.

Local Hero (Forsyth, 1982) uses both an urban and a rural context to discuss its themes. It tells the story of a US oil company's attempt to buy a Scottish village in order to build an oil refinery on the site. Mac MacIntyre is the 'yuppy' sent to the village in order to finalise the deal. The film follows Mac as he changes from Houston 'yuppy' to wanting to live in the Scottish village. In the end, the oil company designates the village and beach a conservation and research area. The rural Scottish community in the film is contrasted with Houston, Texas. This contrast indicates some of the main oppositions of the film. *Local Hero* is organised around a series of oppositions: industry vs ecology, modernity vs tradition, yuppy individualism vs community values and sentimentality vs practicality.

Clichéd ideas about Scotland being a mythological, romantic place are challenged through the depiction of the practicality and realism of the village's inhabitants. Mac is attracted to the villager's community spirit and their realistic value systems. At the end of the film, a compromise is made between the villagers' need for financial gain and the awakening of the oil company to the need for ecology, as well as industry. The Scotland of *Local Hero* is not naive and isolated, but it is a place where an individual's values are reassessed. We come to see that the village community is more realistic and less driven by unattainable goals than the urban environment of Houston. A sense of community is what MacIntyre craves and what he has found lacking in the USA.

> This is a well-presented analysis of the oppositions presented by the film text, with clear indication of their significance.

By contrast, Danny Boyle's 1995 film *Trainspotting** depicts not rural Scotland but urban Edinburgh. The events take place against the backdrop of the heroin culture that existed in parts of this city in the 1980s. Renton, Begbie, Sick Boy and Spud are representatives of the drug-fuelled underclass of the city that exists within its own particular moral world. The film contrasts the Edinburgh of culture, which is often presented in the media, and the Edinburgh that houses the 'worst toilet in Scotland'. According to Renton, 'Scotland is shite', because it is swamped with unemployment and offers little alternative to crime for the protagonists of the film. The characters

in *Trainspotting** have created their own community, with its own hierarchy and value system. Because they have no belief in the ability of the wider community to support them, they have created their own support network. Ironically, this support often comes in the form of drugs. At the end of the film, Renton detaches himself from his friends, knowing that the community offered by them is fundamentally destructive. He does, however, leave money for Spud, in a final supportive act. *Trainspotting** identifies what can happen when a social group feels marginalised and abstracts itself from the main body of society.

Two comparable films are *Small Faces* (Mackinnon, 1996) and *Ratcatcher* (Ramsay, 1999). *Small Faces* is set in Glasgow in the 1960s, in an area populated, and run, by gangs. It follows two brothers who become caught up in the conflict between two rival gangs. *Small Faces* portrays the violence that can exist within an urban Scottish environment. Glasgow is seen as divided — gang territory is sacred and is only accessible to gang members. The disenfranchised youth of *Trainspotting**, who have no focus apart from drugs, are similar to the young people of *Small Faces*, whose identities are formed by their position within a particular gang. The gangs of *Small Faces* have taken the place of traditional social communities. They are violent and destructive, yet offer identity and community to those individuals who crave acceptance.

Ratcatcher is set on an anonymous Scottish housing estate. The families who live in these bleak surroundings suffer from economic hardship. *Ratcatcher* explores the aftermath of a death. James, a young boy from the estate, allows his friend to die, by not saving him from drowning. The rest of the film's narrative follows the consequences of his inaction. *Ratcatcher* depicts Scottish housing estates as anonymous, bleak and depressing. The environment in which the children of the film grow up is harsh and uncompromising. *Ratcatcher* offers an image of what happens to community spirit, when economic hardship becomes a way of life. It contrasts with *Local Hero*, in which economic hardship is not experienced, either by the villagers or those in Houston.

Community is, therefore, not always supportive and community spirit can be seriously affected by factors such as economic depression. The communities within the films I have studied are either alternative communities, created when a group feels marginalised, or communities whose spirit seems to have been broken by the hardships they suffer.

> 🖉 This essay engages with the question and provides a broad range of comments concerning the nature of community. The candidate's points are well substantiated with accurate reference to relevant texts. There is a confidently expressed challenge to stereotypical notions of community and the candidate explores the impact of different communities on characters effectively. The essay has a clear structure, addressing the films systematically, although the comparisons could be made even more explicit.

■ ■ ■

Grade-C answer

Community is important within the films I have studied. There are various different ideas concerning community in my films, some of which are positive and some negative. The films I have chosen to discuss for this essay are *Local Hero* (Forsyth, 1982) and *Trainspotting** (Boyle, 1996).

Local Hero is set in Scotland, in a small village. The people who live in the village have to decide whether or not they are going to accept an offer from a Houston firm to buy the village and turn it into an oil refinery. The village is picturesque and quiet. Everybody knows each other and many of the villagers have more than one job. The village works together and the villagers know each other well. Mac, the representative of the Houston oil firm, comes to the village to agree a deal with the villagers. He is motivated by money and has lived a rich, but lonely, life in Houston. When he arrives in the rural location, however, he begins to reflect on his own life. He sees the free and easy relationships in the village and the slow lifestyle of the villagers. He is attracted by this because it is the opposite of what he has experienced in Houston. At the end of the film, it is Mac who wants to stay in the village. The community spirit has seduced him and made him want to leave his previous life behind.

> ✒ This paragraph needs more discussion of how representation is informed by social and historical context. For instance, Mac's life in Houston is the antithesis of that in Scotland. The candidate does not acknowledge the binary opposition of 1980s consumerism to the (as yet) untainted-by-consumerism society in rural Scotland.

Trainspotting* offers a different representation of community. Renton, Begbie, Spud and Sick Boy are either violent or heroin addicts. They live in a world of drug deals, fights, petty crime and squalid apartments. Renton and his friends do not enjoy the same kind of community as the villagers in *Local Hero*, but they have their own kind of community. They help each other, but do not abide by the laws of a normal society. Renton does attempt to get a life of his own, however. He gets a job and begins to live a life without drugs. This is spoiled when Begbie comes to stay with him and gets him involved in criminal activity. The community represented in *Trainspotting** is founded on drug use, so in the end is not a positive environment.

The films I have studied show community to be a positive thing. Those individuals who live within a community can rely on others for support and protection. However, when people do not have this kind of supportive community around them, they are left lonely and isolated.

> ✒ This essay shows that the candidate is able to choose appropriate films in order to substantiate the points made. There are some interesting points made concerning representation, but these do not often extend beyond character, setting and narrative features. More specific textual references and a more thorough investigation concerning the nature of community would have earned a higher grade.

Question 4

Section A: Comedy

How is gender represented in the films you have studied for this topic?

Grade-A answer

Gender has an important place within the comedy genre. The misunderstandings and complications that often occur in relationships provide scope for plenty of comic scenarios, and the gender characteristics of individuals provide fertile material for comedy too. The representation of gender within comedy films is significant in that it can be used to indicate social attitudes towards men and women that exist outside the film. This essay will focus on the gender representations offered in *East is East* (O'Donnell, 1999), *Bend it Like Beckham* (Chadha, 2002) and *The Full Monty* (Cattaneo, 1997).

> ✍ The candidate shows clear knowledge of the link between representation and social ideologies.

East is East is set in Salford in 1971 and focuses on the Khans, an Asian family living in an otherwise white, working-class community. The relationship between the Asian family and the white community is explored, as is the relationship between the traditional Asian father and his westernised children. The father, George, is Asian and his wife, Ella, is white. Their six children demonstrate the position of people who have mixed-race parents, living in the UK.

The comedy within this film is less overt than the other comedies I will discuss, and the representation of gender is quite complex. Ella's position in the family appears initially to be strong, but as her husband becomes more concerned about his own position she becomes more downtrodden. In the first half of the film, she is seen in comic scenes with her friend discussing men and male/female relationships. She works hard in the family chip shop and is instrumental in attempting to save the deteriorating relationships between her, George and their children. However, when George feels betrayed by his family, he attacks Ella physically, leaving her bruised and muted. In these later scenes, the comic observations that Ella used to deliver are absent. She is at once pivotal within the family unit and yet vulnerable to the shifting self-perception of her husband.

> ✍ This is an excellent exploration of the impact of gender expectations on the character.

The scene in which the Shahs come to arrange the marriages between their daughters and the Khans' sons provides one of the most comic scenes in the film. A piece of 'artwork' depicting female genitalia is used as a prop within this scene to destroy the formality of the meeting. The Shahs find this object repellent and refuse to allow their daughters to marry the Khan sons. At this point, Ella regains her confidence and throws the Shahs out of her house for criticising her family. She is instrumental in allowing her sons to live the western life they want and stands up to George, forcing him to reassess his previous behaviour towards his wife.

✍ This is an interesting comment on the changes that occur within gender representation.

There is a wide range of Asian characters in *Bend it Like Beckham*. This includes those older characters who are highly traditional, young women who are westernised (but still see marriage as their ultimate goal) and a young, gay, Asian man. The film demonstrates the tensions created by attempting to preserve an Asian national culture and religion within a British context. The central character in *Bend it Like Beckham* is an intelligent, young, Asian woman. She is not rebellious, but does want to pursue a sport (football) which her mother finds inappropriate for a young girl. Her father worries that it will both distract her from her studies and put her in a situation of potential racial prejudice. Jess's footballing skills outshine those of the local Asian boys and she confounds their preconceptions of women's sporting abilities. The female characters in *Bend it Like Beckham* are perhaps less supportive than the male characters when it comes to their daughters playing football; the father of Jess's best friend is extremely supportive of his own daughter's interest. The male characters are mixed in their representations. Some are bound by traditional ideas concerning gender and some seem to have no such preconceptions. The attitudes of the female characters are diverse, too. The female footballers challenge stereotypes of female passivity and lack of physical prowess and yet the minor, female, Asian characters are shown to be obsessed with fashion and men.

✍ This shows good understanding of differing gender representations in film.

Another film that plays on gender as part of the comedy is *The Full Monty*. The protagonists are a group unemployed of men struggling to find work in Sheffield, which is suffering economic hardship after the decline of the steel industry. These marginalised men are trying to retain their pride, and react to their situation in different ways. One character cannot tell his wife about his unemployment because he is ashamed, while another has lost interest in sex and his self-esteem. Another character may not be able to see his son if he cannot make his alimony payments. The story uses the unemployment to comic effect, as it follows the men as they form a strip troupe, reversing expectations about women strippers and presenting a different form of masculinity to the feminised men of other male strip troupes. It also makes serious points about gender roles and the damage that occurs when a city can no longer support its workforce.

✍ This is an excellent identification of *The Full Monty*'s portrayal of what can cause social disenfranchisement.

Comedy can engage in discussions concerning gender as effectively as drama. Messages and values are often presented within comic contexts, but this does not mean that they are less serious. The films I have studied indicate the broad range of gender discussions that can be delivered through comedy.

question

 This is a well-argued and accurate essay, which uses a broad range of comedies to discuss the representation of gender. Its argument is confident and fluent, employing textual information to substantiate the points being made. The candidate engages with contextual issues, as well as discussing text-based features. The texts chosen are appropriate and the candidate has selected effective examples from them.

■ ■ ■

Grade-C answer

Gender is an area that causes much debate. Films can represent gender and gender issues positively and negatively. The comedy genre is a useful context in which to make comments on gender, because they can be made in a way that keeps the audience engaged. For this essay, I am going to focus on *East is East* (O'Donnell, 1999) and *The Full Monty* (Cattaneo, 1997).

East is East is set in Salford. The majority of the central characters are Asian and live in a mostly white community. The film discusses the problems that arise when children want to live a western life but their father wishes to retain the traditions of his home country of Pakistan. The mother in this family is white and she often has to act as a peacemaker during family arguments. Ella battles with her husband over the children and in one scene is beaten for not showing him enough support. Ella is in many ways a stereotypical character. She works, but the majority of her time is spent looking after her family. She has little true freedom and is constantly teased by her husband that he will bring his first wife over from Pakistan. The Khans's daughter is less stereotypical. She plays football and fights with her brothers. She does not want an arranged marriage and would prefer to live a western lifestyle. The male characters in *East is East* have very different attitudes. The father is proud and wants to have a dominant position within his family. His sons range from being devoutly Muslim to wanting to reject Islam altogether. The difference between the father and the sons is what causes most of the tensions in the film.

 There is a good evaluation of narrative and gender, but the candidate needs to include social and historical contexts too.

The Full Monty is set in Sheffield and the story concerns a group of unemployed men who are desperate to find work. The men form a strip group in order to attempt to escape from their poverty. The comic scenes within the film revolve around the men's struggles to prove to themselves that they are still masculine. One of the characters has lost interest in sex and one has to lie to his wife about his lost job. The film shows men in a vulnerable position. They have lost their financial power and in some cases have to rely on the women in their lives to support them. Unemployment in Sheffield has made these men feel as if they have no place and the film follows their attempts to regain their confidence.

Both of the films that I have studied discuss both men and women. *East is East* and *The Full Monty* express their attitudes towards gender and gender situations through the characters and the stories told.

🖉 The candidate has chosen appropriate films through which to discuss the representation of gender. As with many grade-C essays, however, most points are made via character observations. The section on *East is East* offers some useful comments concerning the dynamics between the genders, but neither film's context is examined and the points made are fairly simplistic.

Section B

Discuss how a key sequence in your film illustrates the messages and values of the film as a whole.

Grade-A answer

Mike Leigh's film *Secrets and Lies* was made in 1996. It was produced by Channel Four Films (UK), CiBy 2000 (France) and Thin Man Films (UK). Leigh's films are set in the UK and often deal with social problems and individuals who face social deprivation. His settings are often bleak, working-class areas, where individuals battle with financial instability and unemployment, or households where family life is disintegrating under the pressure of internal struggles. Leigh's characters are not glamorous and they often face real struggles in order to achieve happiness. This essay will consider the importance of the first conversation between Hortense and Cynthia in relation to the messages and values of *Secrets and Lies*.

This is an important scene in the film, as it is the first conversation that the two characters have about Hortense's birth. Cynthia initially does not believe that she could be Hortense's mother, but realises during the scene that in fact she is. The scene's importance relates to the title of the film in that the secret of Hortense's birth is revealed.

Hortense and Cynthia are shown in an empty café. The regimented seating around them is empty and no waiting staff can be seen. The significance of this is twofold. The viewer is allowed to concentrate on the conversation between the two with no other visual distraction and the isolation of the pair indicates not only their individual lonely states, but also their isolation with their now shared secret. The two characters are dressed very differently. Hortense wears a black suit, which reflects her mourning, and Cynthia dresses in much lighter and probably cheaper clothes. Their economic and social status is reflected in this aspect of *mise-en-scène* and Cynthia herself comments on the pair's difference. The opening shot of the scene positions the pair to the left of the frame. The emptiness of the café is evident, as is the fact that the women sit on the same side of the table, with Cynthia seated between Hortense and the wall. She appears trapped by the setting and also by the conversation she is having, and this is indicative of her feelings concerning her hopes for life.

> ✍ These are excellent comments concerning the chosen sequence and how the messages and values indicated by micro elements pervade the film as a whole.

There is only one transition in the whole of the scene and this is from the opening shot of Hortense and Cynthia to the left of the frame, to the pair framed symmetrically in mid shot from the opposite side of the café table. The camera has moved closer in order to become more intimate and for the viewer to see the women's expressions more clearly. The camera remains static within this second section of the scene and positions the viewer as if he or she were seated on the other side of the table, listening to the conversation. The body language apparent within this scene is important to the expression of meaning. Hortense seems less anxious than Cynthia, who fidgets with her cigarette and looks away towards the wall when she expresses her 'shame' at not immediately knowing who Hortense's father was. Hortense does not cry, but asks questions concerning the circumstances of her birth. She appears almost numb, in contrast to Cynthia's fits of crying. The women's positions at the table, side by side rather than opposite each other, allow them to occupy separate halves of the same frame. Their connection and their distance at this point in the narrative is thus indicated. This sequence illustrates many of the core preoccupations of the film. The representations of family and social class are discussed by the scene's *mise-en-scène*, as well as its dialogue. The conversation between the pair concerning jobs only serves to make their economic status apparent and the framing of this conversation allows the audience to understand the tensions, expectations, disappointments and problematic dynamics that exist within the families of this film.

Mike Leigh's film is a discussion of family and the impact of socioeconomic factors on family life. The sequence in the café between Hortense and Cynthia illustrates the distance between the two women. They come from entirely different walks of life, they have different educational backgrounds and financial status, and yet they are mother and daughter. *Secrets and Lies* deconstructs traditional representations of the family and offers a narrative that centres on the revelation that given very different family, education and class circumstances, two individuals who are blood relatives can have very different life experiences.

>  This essay identifies the key areas of debate in the focus film clearly. Textual features are identified accurately and used to discuss the wider issues of the film's narrative. The essay includes a clear argument and is expressed in an organised manner. Observations concerning the messages and values of the sequence are well substantiated. This is a confident piece of analysis.

■ ■ ■

Grade-C answer

The James Bond films, especially those made in the 1960s and 1970s, show particular messages and values. Attitudes towards women are reflected in these films, as well as attitudes towards masculinity and nationality. The scene in *Goldfinger* (Hamilton, 1964) when Sean Connery, as James Bond, finds the woman covered in gold paint, is a sequence that demonstrates the messages and values of this film, and will act as the focus of my essay.

Bond has been playing cards with his archenemy Goldfinger. He realises Goldfinger has been cheating with the help of a woman in an apartment overlooking the place where the card game is happening. As is so predictable within the Bond genre, when Bond goes up to the room, he seduces the woman. Her later death is a punishment for her liaison with Bond and is further evidence of Goldfinger's callousness.

> This paragraph indicates an understanding of characterisation, but also needs to illustrate the candidate's knowledge of the ideological position that is evident in the

film and how this position relates to the dominant ideologies in the period the film was made.

As Bond enters the room in this scene, he is struck by the silence. Everything seems quiet and still. There seems to be nothing wrong until he sees the woman dead on the bed. She is glowing and the lighting in the scene initially makes us intrigued, rather than horrified. As Bond moves closer he realises that she has been painted, from head to toe, with gold paint. No skin is left exposed and this is what has caused her death.

The attitude towards women in the Bond films is that they are objects. The woman was killed because she was the 'property' of Goldfinger and betrayed him. Women are either possessions or they are sexual playthings. In many ways, Bond's seduction of the woman was irresponsible, because it caused her death. She had little meaning for him and probably had less for Goldfinger. The fact that the woman is covered in gold paint shows the viewer that she has been branded. She is little more than a sexual toy for both the main male characters in the film.

> Again, these observations should be extended to include debate concerning ideological context. This response is too short, lacks clear textual detail and is inconsistent in its arguments. The candidate does give some indication of how textual features contribute to messages and values, but does not use textual examples to substantiate many of the points. The arguments concerning the messages and values within the film have some degree of accuracy, but are too simplistic.

Section B

In what ways does the opening sequence of your film introduce the viewer to the messages and values of the film?

Grade-A essay

Chicken Run was written and directed by Peter Lord and Nick Park in the year 2000. It was produced by Aardman Animations (UK), Pathé Pictures Ltd (UK) and Dreamworks SKG (US). The film is based on the narrative of John Sturges's 1962 film, *The Great Escape*. It uses the story of a group of hens' confinement in order to explore the themes of entrapment and escape. The opening sequence of the film also introduces the viewer to representations of gender and authority, areas of debate that are explored further in the rest of the film.

The opening sequence of *Chicken Run* also indicates the intertextuality of the film. The sequence presents one of Ginger's failed attempts to escape and subsequent imprisonment in the coal bin. This echoes Steve McQueen's 'cooler king' character's escape attempts in *The Great Escape*. The non-diegetic soundtrack which accompanies the opening credits of the film creates an atmosphere of adventure and excitement. The viewer is immediately introduced into a narrative that promises scenes of high tension and drama, as well as explorations of the key themes within the film.

The opening shot of the film is of the moon. The camera then pans down to frame the chicken run through the fence that imprisons the hens. The setting of the film is thus established as one of a prison and the theme of entrapment is presented to the viewer. The camera then continues to pan away from the fence, eventually resting with a low angle shot of the approaching Mr Tweedy, with one of his dogs. He is presented as threatening and the next, close-up, shot of him checking the padlock on the gate to the chicken run seals his representation as jailer to the hens. The sequence then cuts to a shot of Ginger hiding in the shadows. The *mise-en-scène* provides Ginger with cover, but also establishes a sense of danger and risk. Ginger might be using the shadows to hide, but the darkness also holds the dogs and the farmer. The sequence cuts back to a shot a Mr Tweedy, circling the perimeter fence. This shot also contains the look-out tower, which is at the edge of the fence, another image that reminds the viewer that the chicken run mirrors a prisoner of war camp.

> ✓ The candidate makes excellent links between micro features of the text and messages and values.

Mr Tweedy is shot in fragments for the first few minutes of the film. We see his hand, his boots and shadowed sections of his face. This is a device usually associated with those characters in films who have malevolent intent and in this way Mr Tweedy's negative representation is further confirmed to the viewer. The transitions used in this sequence are cuts and these speed up as the tension of the situation mounts. After the hen gets stuck under the fence and the escape plan begins to founder, the fast cutting creates tension. Ginger attempts to flee from the dogs and Mr Tweedy,

eventually running up the steps towards the farmer's house. She is framed in front of the door, trapped between this door and the dogs. The music is fast paced and builds to a pitch of tension when the dogs move to strike.

At this point in the sequence, however, the pace changes. The front door opens and the non-diegetic sound quietens. The dogs are seen cowering, Ginger's terrified eyes are shown in close-up and the camera begins to pan up the body of Mrs Tweedy. The low angle and upward pan present Mrs Tweedy as powerful. The light source is behind her and she appears to stand out as the authority figure in the scene (and indeed the film). Ginger is thrown into the cooler and one of the last shots of the sequence is a point of view shot of Mr Tweedy's angry face as he closes the door on Ginger. The sequence then cuts to another point of view shot from the hens inside the chicken run, as they watch the angry face of Mr Tweedy looming threateningly.

The opening sequence establishes the pattern of representation that we see explored in the rest of the film. Authority and gender roles are presented in this sequence via the cinematography, editing, sound and *mise-en-scène*. The intertextual elements of *Chicken Run* are highlighted from the outset of the film and the viewer is introduced immediately to the themes of incarceration and escape.

> This essay moves systematically through the sequence, identifying how key features of film form are used to contribute to the film's wider debates. The candidate shows detailed and precise knowledge of the sequence and evaluates representational features in detail. This answer engages directly with the question and uses precise references to the surface textual detail in order to discuss underlying messages and values.

Grade-C answer

Elizabeth (Kapur, 1998) deals with the themes of betrayal, religion and power. The opening scene of the film shows the burning of three Protestants, because their religious nonconformity made them a threat to the state. It introduces the viewer to the main themes of the film.

The film opens with rousing music, which sets the time of the film as just before the Elizabethan era. The opening credits are placed on a red background, with images of crosses. The theme of religion is therefore introduced. The film cuts to a page of old-style writing, again indicating the time in which the film is set. The Protestants are then seen having their heads shaved in preparation for their execution. The soldiers are brutal with the prisoners and the viewer sees blood on the knives being used and blood on the heads of the Protestants. The prisoners are not being treated humanely.

> In order to get a higher grade, this candidate needs to use specific film studies terminology, such as non-diegetic sound.

The film then cuts to an overhead shot of the prisoners walking to the bonfire and their deaths. We see another overhead shot of the three in the middle of the fire. They are vulnerable and terrified. The voices and screams of the prisoners are heard, and at the same time the music and the voices on the soundtrack get louder. The flames grow higher and the prisoners call for the crowd to help them die quicker, because they are in so much pain. The crowd help by throwing twigs onto the fire. As the flames rise, we see the Catholic religious men standing, watching the burning. They do nothing for the people in pain and are happy to punish them for their beliefs.

> The candidate identifies textual detail well, but this needs to be extended into a consideration of how textual elements help illustrate the messages and values of a film.

The opening sequence of *Elizabeth* shows what religion can do. If you did not follow the same religion as the monarchy during this period in history, then you would be punished and killed for your beliefs. The ruling religion is represented by the Catholic religious officials who stand by and do nothing.

> There is a high level of textual detail in this answer. The introduction identifies some of the main themes and concerns of the film accurately. However, the textual detail is not used to discuss the messages and values of the film and many of the well-observed textual points are left without wider debate. The candidate would have received a much higher grade if the messages and values implied within this sequence had been discussed more thoroughly.

Practice questions

Section A: the comparative study

The 1940s: the war and its aftermath

(1) What is the response to war of characters from different classes in the films you have studied?

(2) To what extent do the films you have studied convey a particular sense of regional and/or national identity?

(3) Discuss what you find interesting in the presentation of groups of people — such as families, communities, workers or the military — in the films you have studied for this topic.

Swinging Britain, 1963–73

(1) The 1960s are often referred to as 'swinging'. Do the films you have studied for this topic convey this image?

(2) Do the films you have studied for this topic represent a change in attitudes towards gender and sexuality?

(3) What is the significance of social class in the films you have studied for this topic?

Passions and repressions

(1) Discuss your response to the different representations of relationships in the films you have studied for this topic.

(2) What have you identified as some of the main forms of repression in the films you have studied?

(3) Is passion treated similarly or differently in the films you have studied?

Social and political conflict

(1) How is power represented in the films you have studied?

(2) How have social conflicts affected individuals in the films you have studied for this topic?

(3) How is social class significant to the debates concerning social and/or political conflict in the films you have studied?

Scottish cinema

(1) Does an urban or rural setting make a difference to the representation of national identity in the films you have studied for this topic?

(2) How important are female characters in the films you have studied for this topic?

(3) Discuss the representation of a marginal group in the films you have studied for this topic.

Comedy

(1) Discuss the ways in which comedy is used in your chosen films to discuss wider debates.

(2) How is social class a factor in the comic representations included in the films you have studied?

(3) How important is location within the films you have studied for this topic?

Section B: the single film close study

(1) In what ways does the opening sequence of your film introduce the viewer to the messages and values of the film?

(2) How has information concerning the production context of your close study film increased your understanding and appreciation of the film?

(3) Discuss how a key sequence within your film illustrates the messages and values of the film as a whole.